NORTHWESTERN UNIVERSITY STUDIES
IN THE HUMANITIES

NUMBER 16

NORTHWESTERN UNIVERSITY STUDIES IN THE HUMANITIES NO. 16

FAIR ROSAMOND

A Study of the Development of a Literary Theme

BY

VIRGIL B. HELTZEL

NORTHWESTERN UNIVERSITY

EVANSTON

NORTHWESTERN UNIVERSITY STUDIES · 1947

Open access edition funded by the National Endowment for the Humanities/Andrew W. Mellon Foundation Humanities Open Book Program.

Virgil B. Heltzel. Fair Rosamond: A Study of the Development of a Literary Theme. Evanston, Ill.: Northwestern University Press, 1947.

ISBN 978-0-8101-3844-5 (paper)
ISBN 978-0-8101-3845-2 (ebook)

CONTENTS

CHAPTER PAGE

I. The Genesis of the Story—Fact and Fiction 1

II. The Literary Tradition—Narrative Poetry 14

III. Prose Fiction—Chapbook, Novel, and Tale 39

IV. The Drama: 1693-1840 69

V. The Drama (*continued*): 1840-1938 93

VI. Retrospect 121

Index 133

PREFACE

Few of the old stories deeply rooted in the legendary lore and the history of England have called forth such continuing interest as that of the love of Fair Rosamond and King Henry the Second. For more than six centuries it has captured the fancy of a few men of much, and many of little, literary talent, all the way from the medieval chronicler to the modern poet, dramatist, and novelist. Since the sixteenth century it has been treated in a variety of literary forms—narrative poem, ballad, drama, chapbook, novel, and short story—and has increasingly stimulated the invention of the successive authors who have dealt with it.

This continued literary use of the old legend would alone be enough to invite and justify the attention of the literary historian. The story is peculiarly attractive, however, to the student of thematology interested in the creative processes of literary craftsmen, because he can identify with reasonable accuracy its basic historical elements, observe its early assimilation of folklore-motifs and other fictitious elements in the later chronicle accounts, and study its development from the time when these fabricated versions were first accorded literary treatment to the present day. The consistent interest the story has inspired among professional story-tellers through the centuries is not difficult to explain, for it is one of those "old, unhappy, far-off things" involving royal and historical characters in the eternal triangle. It possesses human interest, and it appeals to the imagination. It has at the same time the virtue of the kind of simplicity that challenges artistic ingenuity and invites widely diversified artistic conception and treatment.

Biographers and historians have done something toward establishing the historical basis of the story, but no study has been given to its literary development. In the following pages I propose to follow the entire course of its growth in English literature. I shall sketch what is known of its historical basis, indicate such sources and influences as I can discover in its growth, follow the development of artistic departures, attempt to estimate the special contribution of the individual author, and explain as best I can the role of the culture of each age in shaping the story to its own taste and literary practice. In the course of the study, I may add, I have been sensible of the repetition involved in the almost endless synopses I have felt obliged to give, as well as of the difficulties of making them accurately representative of their originals, But the student must apply to all his specimens the same standards of evaluation, and I know of no other method of presentation which would be fair to the reader and at the same time preserve him from danger of bewilderment.

For the sake of consistency in my comments on the story, I have had to choose between two spellings of the name of the heroine. Except in titles and quoted passages in which her name appears as *Rosamund* or as a variation of that spelling, I have used the form *Rosamond,* because it is favored by usage in the tradition and is etymologically the more correct form. The derivation of the word from the Latin phrase *rosa mundi* is evidently nothing more than a poetical fancy. I have followed traditional usage also in normalizing such variants as *Elinor, Elenor, Eleanora,* etc., to *Eleanor*.

I wish to make grateful acknowledgment of my debt for special services or loans to the following institutions: the British Museum, the Huntington Library, the Library of Congress, the Boston Public Library, and the libraries of Harvard University, the University of Michigan, and the University of Texas. I am of course especially indebted to those libraries in which I carried on most of my research: Deering Library of Northwestern University, the Newberry Library, the Chicago Public Library, and the Libraries of the University of Chicago. My thanks are due also to Mrs. Anne Welch Haines for inspecting a number of the later versions of the story; to Miss Dorothy Hutchison, of Deering Library, for useful reference work; to my lamented friend, the late Professor Frederick H. Heidbrink; and to my colleagues, Professors Frederic E. Faverty, Leon Howard, and Arthur H. Nethercot. To Professor Hardin Craig I extend cordial thanks for helpful reading of the manuscript. Finally, I owe a special debt to Professor John W. Spargo, editor of the Northwestern University Studies, whose careful reading of my manuscript has forestalled numerous errata.

Evanston, Illinois V. B. H.
May 17, 1946

CHAPTER I

THE GENESIS OF THE STORY—FACT AND FICTION

I

THE STORY of Fair Rosamond, as it recurs in the earliest versions, when reduced to its essential elements, may be outlined somewhat as follows: Rosamond Clifford, destined to be known to posterity as "Fair Rosamond" because of her exceeding beauty, became the mistress of Henry the Second, King of England, by whom she had two sons. To protect her from the increasing jealousy of his consort, Queen Eleanor of Aquitaine, King Henry secluded her in a palace which he had caused to be built at or near Woodstock—a bower surrounded by an intricate labyrinth or maze to which he alone (and sometimes a keeper) had the clue. Taking advantage of Henry's absence from England, the Queen by one means or another threaded the maze, and, confronting Rosamond, compelled her to choose between a dagger and a bowl of poison in expiation of her sin. Rosamond chose to drink the poison, and her body was interred in Godstow Nunnery. For her act of treachery Queen Eleanor was imprisoned by the king for the remainder of his reign. Not always a part of the story is the account of how when Hugh, Bishop of Lincoln, upon a visitation to Godstow in 1191, found the nuns performing special rites over Rosamond's body, he ordered it to be removed from the church; and how later the nuns carefully collected the bones and gave them proper burial, and how for her a tomb was erected bearing a curious epitaph.

How much of this story, which was variously elaborated later, is historical cannot be determined with certainty. Fair Rosamond can be identified as one of six children of Walter de Clifford[1] (d. 1190?) who was a knight possessed of several manors and a benefactor of several monasteries, among them Godstow itself.[2] That she was the mistress of Henry II is plainly reported by contemporary writers.[3]

[1] See the history of the Clifford family in R. W. Eyton, *Antiquities of Shropshire*, 12 vols. (London, 1854-60), V, 146ff.

[2] See *Vict. County History of Oxford*, II, 71-2; Dugdale, *Monasticon*, ed. Caley, Ellis, and Bandinel, 6 vols. (London, 1817-30), IV, 357ff., and Appendix xv, p. 366.

[3] Cf. *Gesta Regis Henrici Secundi Benedicti Abbatis*, ed. William Stubbs, II (London, 1867), 231-2: the nuns of Godstow "dixerunt ei [i. e., Hugh of Lincoln] quod illud erat sepulcrum Rosaemundae, quam Henricus rex Angliae tantum dilexerat, quod pro amore ejus domum illam, quae prius erat pauper et mendicans multis et magnis redditibus ditaverat, et nobilibus aedificiis decoraverat." Roger de Hoveden, in his *Chronica*, ed. Stubbs, III (London, 1870), 167-8, reporting the same incident, says that Rosamond "exstiterat amica Henrici regis Angliae." Giraldus Cambrensis, in *De principis instructione liber*, ed. George F. Warner (London, 1891), p. 232, refers to Rosamond as one "quam rex adulterinis amplexibus nimis adamaverat."

According to Giraldus Cambrensis (1146?-1220?) in his *De principis instructione,* after the suppression of the great rebellion (September, 1174), Henry, having imprisoned his queen, openly declared his illicit relationship with Rosamond:

> Biennali vero clade sedata, cessantibus quoque plagis et persecutionibus, . . . ad solitam vitiorum voraginem vel, quoniam "proclivior usus in pejora datur," longe deteriorem incorrigibiliter inclinavit. Et, ut aliis omissis unum in medium proponamus, olim incarcerata sponsa sua Alienora regina in poenam forte maritalis excidii primi consensusque secundi, qui adulter antea fuerat occultus, effectus postea manifestus, *non mundi* quidem *rosa* juxta falsam et frivolam nominis impositionem, sed *immundi verius rosa* vocata palam et impudenter abutendo.[4]

This account is repeated by later writers, who add that soon after the king's open acknowledgment of her she died ("sed illa cito obiit") and was buried in Godstow Nunnery.[5] By the year 1274 it may be inferred from the verdict of the jurors of Corfham, as Archer points out, that "it was already a popular story on a Clifford manor that Rosamond Clifford had been the mistress of Henry II."[6]

The belief that Rosamond had two sons by Henry, viz., Geoffrey, later archbishop of York, and William Longsword, later earl of Salisbury, is not noticed by any writer before Ferne (1586), and although various later writers (e.g., Hume, Carte, Lyttelton, Benington, Eyton) accepted the tradition as fact, it is very likely that it had its origin in the late sixteenth or early seventeenth centuries.[7]

All early writers who make mention of Rosamond's death agree that she was buried at Godstow, and the story, first told in the *Gesta Regis Henrici Secundi,* sometimes attributed to Benedict, Abbot of Peterborough, is repeated with minor variations by later chroniclers. According to this account, St. Hugh, Bishop of Lincoln, upon a visitation to Godstow Nunnery in 1191, upon entering the chapel, ubi [cum] ante

[4] Pp. 165-6. For identification of a veiled reference to Rosamond in the words I have italicized, see quotation from Higden below, p. 6.

[5] Higden, *Polychronicon,* ed. Joseph Rawson Lumby, Rolls Series, VIII (London, 1882), 52-4; Henry Knighton, *Chronica,* ed. Roger Twysden (London, 1652), p. 2395; Brompton, *Chronicon,* ed. Roger Twysden (London, 1652), p. 1151. Eyton, *op. cit.,* V, 147, places the date of Rosamond's death at "*circa* 1175-6," and this has been accepted by most writers.

[6] *Hundred Rolls of Ed. I,* II, 93-94: "Dicunt quod [Corfham erat in] antiquo dominico Regum, set Henricus Rex pater Johannis Regis dedit [Waltero] de Clifford pro amore Rosamundae filiae suae." Quoted in T. A. Archer's article, "Rosamond Clifford," in *DNB.*

[7] For a brief statement of this problem, a rather irrelevant one here, see *ibid,*

magnum altare prolixius orasset, vidit ibi sepulcrum quoddam ante altare panno serico coopertum, et cum lampadibus ardentibus cereos circumstantes, quod in magna habebatur reverentia a praedictis monialibus. Et quaesivit a circumstantibus cujus esset sepulcrum illud, quod in tanta habebatur reverentia. Et dixerunt ei quod illud erat sepulcrum Rosaemundae, quam Henricus rex Angliae tantum dilexerat, quod pro amore ejus domum illam, quae prius erat pauper et mendicans multis et magnis redditibus ditaverat, et nobilibus aedificiis decoraverat, [ac] redditus magnos eidem ecclesiae contulerat ad inveniendum [lumen] illus indeficiens circa sepulcrum illud.

Quibus episcopus ait, "Tollite eam hinc, quia scortum fuit, et amor ille qui inter regem et illam fuit illicitus erat et adulterinus. Et sepelite eam cum aliis mortuis extra ecclesiam, ne Christiana religio vilescat; et ut exemplo illius caeterae mulieres exterritae caveant sibi ab illicitis [et] adulterinis concubitibus." Et illae fecerunt sicut praeceperat eis episcopus, et tollentes eam sepelierunt extra ecclesiam.[8]

There is in contemporary documents no hint of any foul play in the death of Rosamond—no real evidence to support the traditional beliefs either that Queen Eleanor's jealousy led to an act of vengeful reprisal or that her imprisonment was in punishment of any act of violence against her rival. That the queen could have had any part in the death of Rosamond seems to be refuted by the fact that for her abettal of her children's conspiracy and rebellion against King Henry she was a closely guarded prisoner from 1173, several years before Rosamond's death, to 1185. Agnes Strickland's conjecture as to the origin of the association of the imprisonment of the queen with Rosamond's death deserves mention. She points out that Rosamond's death, about 1176, coincided roughly, in the folk mind, with the imprisonment of the queen. "This coincidence," she continues,

revived the memory of romantic incidents connected with Henry's love for Rosamond Clifford. The high rank of the real object of the queen's jealousy at that time, and the circumstances of horror regarding Henry's profligacy, as the seducer of the princess Alice, her son's wife, occasioned a mystery at court which no one dared to define. The common people, in their endeavors to guess this state secret, combined the death of the poor penitent at Godstow with Eleanor's imprisonment, and thus the report was raised that Eleanor had killed Rosamond. To these causes we trace the disarrangement of the chronology in the story of Rosamond, which has cast doubt on the truth of her adventures.[9]

[8] II, 231-2. Cf. Roger de Hoveden, *Chronica,* ed. Stubbs, III, 167-8; Walter of Coventry, *Memoriale,* ed. Stubbs, II (London, 1873), 14.

[9] *Lives of the Queens of England from the Norman Conquest,* 8 vols. (Philadelphia, 1893), I, 268-9. Cf. Giraldus, *De principis instructione liber,* ed. Warner, p. 232.

Woodstock Park with its royal palace was already in existence before the reign of Henry II,[10] and Henry, who was frequently in residence at the palace, may have entertained or secluded Rosamond there. There is no contemporary evidence, however, that any manor house, bower, or chamber was built by him specifically for the purpose. Nevertheless, there is reason to believe that a generation or two after the death of Henry II, at least one room at Winchester was known as "Camera Rosamundae." Thomas Warton mentions that "In the pipe-rolls of Henry the Third we have this notice, A.D. 1257. 'Infra portam castri et birbecanam, etc. ab exitu Camera Rosamundae usque capellam sancti Thomae in Castro Wynton.'" Warton says he once supposed this to be a chamber in Winchester Castle "painted with the figure or some history of fair Rosamond. But a Rosamond-Chamber was a common apartment in the royal castles, perhaps in imitation of her bower at Woodstock, literally nothing more than a *chamber*, which yet was curiously constructed and decorated, at least in memory of it. The old prose paraphrast of the Chronicle of Robert of Gloucester says, 'Boures hadde the Rosamonde a bout in Engelonde, which this kynge [Henry II.] for hir sake made: atte Waltham bishope's, in the castelle of Wynchester, atte park of Fremantel, atte Martelston, atte Woodestoke, and other fele places.'"[11] It is not necessary to believe that Henry made these many "bowers" in which to entertain Rosamond. It is possible that to commemorate Rosamond, it may have become customary or fashionable for later generations, to whom her story had become well known, to designate some special chamber by her name.[12] In partial support of the prose paraphrast quoted by Warton may be cited a letter from Edward III (1312-77) to William de Montacute, in which he orders "various repairs at his manor of Woodstock; and

[10] The royal palace and Woodstock Park were constructed by Henry I, and according to John Rous (Ross) "parcus erat primus parcus Angliae . . . et constructus erat circa xiiii. regni hujus regis [i.e., Henrici I], vel parum post." (*Historia regum Angliae*, ed. Hearne, 2nd ed. [Oxford, n.d.], p. 138.) Cf. Camden, *Britannia* (London, 1587), p. 230: "Aedes hic [i.e., at Woodstock] sunt regiae magnificentiae plenae, ab Henrico primo constructae, qui etiam viuarium amplissimum saxeo muro incinctum adiunxit."

[11] *History of English Poetry*, 4 vols. (London, 1824), II, 139-40, note. The passage quoted is to be found also in Dugdale, *Monasticon*, IV, 358, note.

[12] At a much later date the name of Rosamond was so associated with places which could have had no connection with her. I may cite "Rosamond's Pond," applied in the eighteenth century to a pond in the southwest corner of St. James's Park, near Buckingham Gate. It was a well-known place of meeting for lovers, and of suicides by disappointed maidens. See Tom Brown, *Amusements*, ed. Arthur L. Hayward (London, 1927), p. 44; Steele, in *The Tatler*, ed. George A. Aitken, 4 vols. (London, 1898-99), Nos. 60, 114, 170. In no. 213, Tom Springley pretends an assignation with a married woman at the Pond, when he is actually going to evening prayers. The Pond was filled up in 1770.

that the house *beyond the gate in the new wall* be built again, and that same chamber, called Rosamond's chamber, to be restored as before, and crystal plates, and marble, and lead to be provided for it."[13] Upon this passage Strickland has this comment: "Here is indisputable proof that there was a structure called Rosamond's chamber, distinct from Woodstock palace yet belonging to its domain, being a building situated beyond the park wall. Edward III. passed the first years of his marriage principally at Woodstock, therefore he well knew the localities of the place; which will agree with the old chroniclers, if we suppose Rosamond's residence was approached by a tunnel under the park wall." That Woodstock had a maze, however, would not necessarily mean that it had been made specifically to conceal Rosamond, for, as W. H. Matthews points out, "contrivances of the kind described in the legend of Rosamond may have been in existence not only in Henry's time but even in the previous century."[14] In fact, the great wall enclosing Woodstock Park[15] could have offered sufficient mystery to the folk mind to have become transformed into a labyrinth.

A statement can now be made as to the historical elements in the story of Henry and Rosamond as developed by the chroniclers. We may be reasonably certain a) that "Fair Rosamond" was Rosamond Clifford, daughter of Walter de Clifford, b) that she was the mistress of Henry II after (if not before) his marriage to Eleanor of Aquitaine, c) that the queen, however she may have felt about her husband's infidelity, could not have poisoned her, but d) that soon after Henry's open acknowledgment of Rosamond as his mistress, Rosamond died and was buried at Godstow.

There is, on the other hand, no real evidence that Rosamond had any children by the king, nor that he had a palace built specifically to protect her from the vengeance of the queen, though there is some evidence in early tradition for associating Rosamond's name with a specific chamber or bower at Woodstock and for believing that a maze or labyrinth may have been some part of the grounds or buildings of the royal residence there.

II

There now remains the task of tracing the gradual accumulation of unhistorical accretions that clustered increasingly about the famous

[13] Quoted from *Foedera,* IV, 629, by Strickland, I, 269, note.

[14] *Mazes and Labyrinths* (London, 1922), p. 112. Matthews thinks that Brompton's description of the bower (mirabilis architecturae cameram operi Daedalino similem) suggests "a labyrinth of an architectural kind, perhaps like that . . . built at Ardres by Louis of Bourbourg . . . in the twelfth century" (p. 165)—"a nearly inextricable labyrinth, containing recess within recess, room within room, turning within turning" (p. 111).

[15] See above, p. 4, note 10.

pair to the end of the sixteenth century, when, the materials having become adequate and inviting, the first of many attempts was made to give artistic treatment to the story. The first of the old chroniclers to indulge in what may be called a slight embroidery of historical fact is Ranulf Higden, who wrote probably before the middle of the fourteenth century. He repeats Giraldus's report[16] of Henry's declaration of his relationship to Rosamond, referring to the king as one who "had prisoned his wif Eleanore the queene," to use Trevisa's translation, and who, though he "was preveliche a spouse brekere, leveth now openliche in spousebreche, and is nought aschamed to mysuse the wenche Rosameund." But he adds, from a source he does not identify, that Henry had a chamber made at Woodstock to hide Rosamond from the queen, gives her epitaph, and describes a marvellous coffer the king had given her:

> Huic nempe puellae spectatissimae fecerat rex apud Wodestok mirabilis architecturae cameram opere Daedalino sinuatam, ne forsan a regina facile deprehenderetur, sed illa cito post obiit, et apud Godestowe juxta Oxoniam in capitulo monialium sepulta est cum tali epitaphio. *Versus de Rosamunda.*
>
> Hic jacet in tumba Rosa mundi non rosa munda,
> Non redolet sed olet quod redolere solet.
>
> Cista ejusdem puellae vix bipedalis mensurae sed mirabilis architecturae ibidem cernitur, in qua conflictus pugilum, gestus animalium, volatus avium, saltus piscium, absque hominis impulsu conspiciuntur.[17]

Each of these three new elements in the story—the chamber at Woodstock, the epitaph, and the coffer—calls for individual attention.

To Trevisa, the translator of Higden, the chamber was "of wonder craft, wonderliche i-made by Dedalus werke." It will be noticed that in his translation he omits the important meaning in *sinuatam,* which with its suggestion of a "winding" or "curved" chamber (*cameram*) may be responsible for later elaborations of the conception of a maze or labyrinth. The account by Higden is copied without variation by Henry Knighton[18] and John Brompton,[19] and alluded to in minor intervening chronicles. In his *Concordance of Histories* (1516) Robert Fabyan seems somewhat intrigued by the idea of the "howse of a wonder workynge."

> But yet [after Eleanor's imprisonment and Henry's victory over the Scottish king] he lefte not the company of the forenamed Rosamounde,

[16] See above, p. 2.

[17] *Polychronicon . . . with the English translations of John Trevisa,* ed. Joseph Rawson Lumby, Rolls Series 41, vol. VIII (London, 1882), pp. 52-4.

[18] *Cronica,* p. 2395.

[19] *Chronicon,* p. 1151.

> to the which wenche he had made an howse of a wonder workynge, so that noo creature, man or woman, myght wyn to her, but if he were instructe by the kynge, or suche as were ryght secret with hym, touchinge that matter. This howse, after some wryters, was named labor intus, or Deladus [sic] werke, or howse, which is to mean, after moost exposytours, an howse wrought lyke unto a knot in a garden, called a mase.[20]

Here, for the first time, we have a definite emphasis on the means taken by the king to make it impossible for anybody except himself, "or such as were ryght secret with hym," to reach Rosamond's chamber. A "howse wrought lyke unto a knot in a garden, called a mase," begins to take form as a device against intruders.

In 1569, Richard Grafton cites Higden as his source, but apparently takes some freedom in his description of "a Bowre or chamber, which was so artificially wrought and was such a laberinth and so full of turnings, dores, and wayes most curiously devysed and made, that it was not possible without teaching to come to any that was therein, and that the same is called at this day Rosamonds Bowre."[21] Holinshed (1578, 1587) combines in his explanation of the house at Woodstock the ideas of both Fabyan and Grafton, following them *verbatim.*[22] Michael Drayton, bringing imagination and immediate interest to the subject, which figures in his "Annotations" to the Epistle of *Rosamond to King Henry the Second,* describes the intricacies of the bower as follows:

> *Rosamonds* Labyrinth, whose Ruines, together with her Well, being paved with square Stone in the bottome, and also her Tower, from which the Labyrinth did runne (are yet remaining) was altogether under ground, being Vaults arched and walled with Bricke and Stone, almost inextricably wound one within another; by which, if at any time her Lodging were laid about by the Queene, shee might easily avoid Perill eminent, and if neede be, by secret Issues take the Ayre abroad, many Furlongs, round about *Woodstocke* in *Oxfordshire,* wherein it was situated.[23]

Drayton's parenthetical remark that the labyrinth, well, and tower still remain was first printed in 1597. Camden, however, in 1586, had

[20] *The New Chronicles of England and France,* ed. Henry Ellis (London, 1811), pp. 275-7.

[21] *Chronicles at Large,* ed. Sir Henry Ellis, 2 vols. (London, 1809), I, 214.

[22] Chronicles (London, 1587) III, 115. Cf. also Stowe, *Annales* (London, 1631), p. 154; William Camden, *Britannia,* ed. Richard Gough, 4 vols. (London, 1806), II, 4; John Speed, *History of Great Britain* (London, 1611), p. 471.

[23] *Works,* ed. Hebel, 5 vols. (London, 1931-41), II, 139.

written of the labyrinth as no longer in existence: "qui hodie nusquam apparet."[24]

The epitaph, the second of the additions to the story as told by contemporary chroniclers, first appears, as has been noticed, in Higden's *Polychronicon,* where we are informed that Rosamond was buried at Godstow "cum tali epitaphio:

> Hic jacet in tumba Rosa mundi non rosa munda,
> Non redolet sed olet quod redolere solet,"

which Trevisa translates freely as "Here lieth in tombe the rose of the world, nought a clene rose; it smelleth nought swete, but it stinketh, that was wont to smelle ful swete."[25] This epitaph affords the first hint that we may have here a possible influence of a much older well-known story of another character of the same name—Rosamunda, queen of the Lombards, who died of poison in the sixth century. An identical epitaph, according to Bernardino Corio, fifteenth-century historian of Milan, was to be found in his time on the tomb of the Lombard queen.[26] The story of Rosamunda, first told by Paulus Diaconus (*Historia,* lib. ii, ch. 28-30) of the eighth century, without the epitaph, however, apparently had wide currency during the Middle Ages. What is more pertinent in this connection is that it was retold in full by Higden himself in the *Polychronicon,*[27] for the first time, so far as I can learn, in any chronicle dealing with Henry and his Rosamond. Who is responsible for this not improbable confusion is beyond conjecture, but the *Polychronicon,* which all succeeding chroniclers who deal with the Rosamond story lean upon heavily, contains in itself all the ingredients necessary for such a confusion.[28]

The epitaph is repeated by all chroniclers who draw from Higden or from one another, but nothing of significance is added.[29] John Leland, who is the first writer to give any new information about Rosamond's tomb, writes from what appears to be firsthand knowledge when he says, "Rosamundas tumbe at Godestow nunnery was taken up a late,

[24] *Britannia* (London, 1587), p. 231.

[25] *Op. cit.,* VIII, 53-55.

[26] *L'historia di Milano* (Venice, 1554), I, 20-1. The inscription on the tomb of Rosamunda is discussed by one "W. D." in N. & Q., 2nd Series, X (1860), 88.

[27] V, 370ff.

[28] For further discussion of the points of similarity between the two stories, see below, pp. 18-19 and note 9.

[29] I.e., *in loc. cit.,* Knyghton; Brompton ("ubi talis suprascriptio invenitur"); Fabyan, who tries his hand at a rhyme-royal Englishing of the epitaph; Grafton, who quotes Fabyan's rendering; Holinshed, who draws from Grafton; Stow; Camden, who translates the epitaph in two couplets; and Speed, who produces a couplet translation. Henry Parker, in *A Compendiouse Treatise Dyalogue of Dives & Pauper* (London, 1493), sig. t[iii] v., says the king himself composed the Latin verses.

it ad [had?] a stone, with this inscription, *Tumba Rosamundae,* her bones were closid in lede, and withyn that the bones were closid yn leder. When it was openid ther was a very swete [smell] cam owt of it.

"Ther is a crosse hard by Godestow with this inscription,

> *Qui meat hac oret signum salutis adoret*
> *Utque sibi detur veniam Rosamunda precetur.*"[30]

It is surprising that Leland, who must have known the earlier accounts and must have had some close acquaintance with what happened "a late," quotes an entirely different inscription on a cross hard by without making any mention of the *Hic jacet* first recorded by Higden, unless the reference to the sweet smell may emit some faint odor of the famous epitaph! Since Higden gives no indication that he had actually seen the epitaph, one can doubt that it ever existed at Godstow. On the other hand, if we are to assume that it did exist at Godstow, there is good reason for the belief that it may have been derived directly or indirectly from the tomb of Rosamunda of the Lombards.

The last new ingredient introduced by Higden—the marvellous "litel cofre," as Trevisa puts it, "scarsliche of two foot long, i-made by a wonder craft, that is yit i-seyn there. Thereynne it semeth that geantes fighten, bestes stertelleth, foules fleeth and fisches mooven with oute manis hond meovynge"—may be disposed of briefly, because the account of the casket or coffer is tied to that of the epitaph, and is handed down from chronicler to chronicler in much the same way. Beyond Higden's assertion, "cista . . . mirabilis ibidem cernitur," there is no evidence that such a casket was to be seen at Godstow.

Whatever vestige of historical fact may have survived in Higden's assertions concerning the maze, the epitaph, and the coffer, there is almost certainly none in that later feature of the story which consigns Rosamond to death by poison at the hand of a jealous and vengeful queen. But the beginnings for such an episode in the story are to be found in Higden, because the curious *camera* with its Daedelian work was contrived, so we are told, "ne forsan a regina facile deprehenderetur"—an excellent point of departure for the motive of jealousy and the execution of vengeance upon the unfortunate rival. As a matter of fact, these motives were already in existence at the time of Higden's writing, in a story of a sufficiently lurid nature to have invited incorpo-

[30] *Itinerary,* ed. Lucy Toulmin Smith (London, 1907), I, 328. A variation of this inscription, with translation, is given by John Speed (*History,* ed. 1611, p. 471):

> "Qui meat hac, oret, Signumque salutis adoret,
> Utq; tibi detur requies Rosamunda, precetur.
> All you which passe this way, This Crosse adore, and pray,
> That Rosamund's Soule, may True rest possess for Aye."

ration into the main stream of tradition. They appear in *The French Chronicle of London (Croniques de London, depuis l'An 44 Henry III. jusqu' à l'An Edw. III.)*, which was compiled, so its editor thinks, "about the middle of the fourteenth century," and "appears to be an abridgement of some romance or legend." By a confusion of identity not uncommon in stories of folk origin, the royal avenger is made not Eleanor of Aquitaine but Eleanor of Provence, the queen of Henry III. The gruesome story tells how the queen had Rosamond, the king's concubine, taken prisoner, disrobed, placed between two fires, and afterward bled to death in a bath. As soon as the blood was flowing, we are told,

> vint une autre escomengée sorceresse, si porta deus horribles crapaudes sure un troboille, si les mist sure les mameles au gentile damoisele, et taunttost seiserent let mameles et comenserent à leiter[31] . . . Et totdis les ordres crapaudes les mameles de la tresbele damoisele leterent, et la roygne riaunt totdis le moka, et out graunt joye en queor, qe ele estoit ensy vengée de Rosamonde. Et quaunt ele fu morte, si fist prendre le corps et en une ordre fossée entrer, et les crapaudes oveske le corps.

But when the king heard the news of what the queen had done, he was greatly angered and sorely aggrieved. By torturing the evil sorceress he found out the truth and rode toward Woodstock, for in order to hide her deed the queen was conveying the body to Godstow Nunnery. On his way, he came upon the body in a chest strongly bound with iron, which, being opened, exposed to view the horrible sight of the tortured body of his beloved. He swore a great oath that he would avenge the filthy felony that had been done the gentle damsel through jealousy. " 'Allas! dolente!' fist il, 'douce Rosamonde, unkes ne fust ta pere,si douce ne si bele creature ne fust unkes trovée.' " And he prayed for her soul. He ordered the body to be taken to Godstow, and "là fist faire son sepulture en ceste religiouse mesoun de nonaynes, et illuques ordeina tresze chapeleins à chaunter pur l'alme de la dite Rosamonde taunqe le siecle dure. En ceste religious mesoun de Godestowe, vous die pur verité, gist la bele Rosamonde ensevely. Verray dieux omnipotent de s'alme en eit mercy. Amen."[32]

Although we have here no maze, no suggestion that a secluded Rosamond had to be surprised to be taken, we do have the motive of jealousy and the murder—true enough, not by dagger or poison, as in later versions, but by something more terrible, the worse for Queen Eleanor's reputation! I have not found a repetition of this story,[33]

[31] For references to information about this piece of witchcraft, see G. L. Kittredge, *Witchcraft in Old and New England* (Cambridge, Mass., 1929), p. 497, note 40.

[32] Ed. George James Aungier, Camden Society, XXVIII (London, 1844), pp. 3-5.

[33] But see a possible influence of the story in Daniel, below, p. 18.

but the use of the toads may account for her presence in Henry Parker's report of the death of Rosamond and of what thereafter ensued. In his version, Rosamond was so beautiful that after her death (which occurred while the king was absent from the country) the king "wolde se the body in the graue. And whanne the graue was opened, there sate an orrible tode vpon hir breste bytwene hir teetys: and a foule adder begirt hir body aboute in the midle, and she stanke so that the kyng ne non other might stonde to se that orryble sight." To Parker this "fact" explains the peculiar nature of the epitaph, for "Thanne the kynge dyde shette ayen the graue, and dyde wryte these veersis upon the graue." Then follows the Latin epitaph.[34]

With the introduction of the motive of vengeance provided by the *French Chronicle*, we have on record for the first time all the essentials for a story of conflict—a triangular love affair ending in tragedy. In Higden, as we have seen, everything is ripe for the entrance of the jealous queen to ferret out her rival and do away with her. Such a role had no doubt very early been assigned to the queen by the folk, and the account in the *French Chronicle*, almost certainly based on oral tradition, had even in Higden's time fully provided it. But neither in Higden nor in any of the succeeding chroniclers who freely drew from him for their materials does anything happen. Except for the *French Chronicle* version, no writer before the sixteenth century assigns to Queen Eleanor a definite role in the affair. The first writer to do so was Robert Fabyan, who gives "ye comon fame" as his source of information. Writing in 1516, he says "Ye comon fame tellyth, y^{t} lastly the quene wañe to her [i.e. Rosamond] by a clever clewe of threde, or sylke, and delte with her in suche maner, that she lyved not longe after. Of the maner of her deth spekyth nothynge myn auctour."[35] Holinshed makes the means by which the queen got at Rosamond a little more definite, saying "the common report of the people is, that the queene in the end found hir out by a silken thread, which the king had drawne after him out of hir chamber with his foot, and dealt with hir in such sharpe and cruell wise, that she lived not long after."[36] John Speed, writing as late as 1611, appears to have known something of both the "burning jealousie in the Queene, and [the] fatall ruine" of Rosamond, but he suggests only that "had not Fate, and Heavens revenge on Adultery, shewed the way, the enraged Queen had not so soone beene rid of her Rivall, nor that wanton Dame of her life."[37]

[34] *A Compendiouse Treatise* (London, 1493), sig. t^{iii} verso.

[35] *The New Chronicle of England and France*, ed. Henry Ellis (London, 1811), p. 277. Grafton (ed. 1569, pp. 214-15) follows this account. Cf. Stow, *Annales* (ed. 1631), p. 154.

[36] *Chronicles* (London, 1587), III, 115.

[37] P. 471. See also Fuller, in his *Worthies*, ed. John Nichols, 2 vols. ([London],

Thus, in none of the accounts except that of the *French Chronicle* is the manner of Rosamond's death specified. For that we must look to the first literary treatments of the story by William Warner and Samuel Daniel.

From their point of vantage, one might ask, what was the nature of the materials available for artistic treatment of the story of Henry and Rosamond? It is significant that for a century and a half after the event, during which time some report of the affair was no doubt often repeated in oral tradition, there is no reason to believe that any fictitious elements were placed on record, but phrases employed by sixteenth-century chroniclers—"the common fame telleth," "the common report of the people"—indicate that some sort of oral version of the story was well known as late as Elizabethan times. On the other hand, writers of chronicles, who were no doubt serious men, were slow to accept more than certain features of the legend. Even the presumably unhistorical additions made by Ranulf Higden about the middle of the fourteenth century were insufficient for more than a starting-point for a story, because in his report he provides no definite conflict. But that oral tradition had already fabricated motivation and conflict and denouement is evident from the account in the *French Chronicle* (before 1350). Of the several additions made by Higden—the labyrinth, the epitaph, and the coffer—the epitaph in all probability had derived ultimately from some version of the well-known story of Rosamunda, queen of the Lombards, just as from the same source the earliest literary versions took over the tenaciously persistent idea that Rosamond died of poisoning. Higden's brief account of the labyrinth, somewhat embroidered by sixteenth-century chroniclers, may have resulted from association in oral tradition of an actual maze—which could have been some part of Woodstock Palace, as such contrivances were of many another palace in the period[38]—with oral or recorded accounts which form an apparently unbroken tradition from ancient times.[39] It is hardly necessary, however, to recall anything as ancient as the Theseus and Ariadne story as a possible inspiration for the use of a clue in threading a labyrinth. Perhaps a much more recent type of folk tale offers more promise as a general source of the idea. I have in mind a tale associated with the *Wildfrau* of German folklore—a tale widely disseminated during the medieval and early modern periods.[40]

1811), I, 455, who does not venture any more specific information as to the manner of Rosamond's death than does Speed: "By some device she got accesse unto her, and caused her death."

[38] See Matthews, *passim,* but especially chapters xiv, xv, xix.

[39] *Ibid.*, chapters ii-viii.

[40] For a study of the tale, see "Traces of a *Wildfrau* Story in Erasmus," in *PQ.*, VIII (1929), 348-54.

It is, in part, the story of a wife who, becoming suspicious of her husband's unsatisfactorily explained absences from home, manages, by means of a clue of thread or by some other such device, to find her way through the forest to a retreat where she discovers him asleep with a *Wildfrau.* There is, it is true, no motive of jealousy present–only anxiety and suspicion–and the story ends on forgiveness rather than in the more natural act of revenge. There is, moreover, no real evidence that the tale was ever current in England, although it was known in France, which amounted to much the same thing in the twelfth and thirteenth centuries. My sole contention is that here is evidence that the folk were as capable of supplying a clue of thread as they were of transforming a palatial maze into a marvellous labyrinth. What is more to our immediate purpose in the next chapter is that, by what may be mere coincidence, a literary version of this story–without the clue, however–appears in William Warner's *Albion's England,*[41] where, together with his story of Fair Rosamond, it is related to Queen Mary to suggest to her what conduct to pursue in dealing with Philip, who had fallen in love with a baker's daughter in Brabant.

[41] Bk. viii, ch. xlii.

CHAPTER II

THE LITERARY TRADITION—NARRATIVE POETRY

WHO MUST be accorded the honor of having first given the story of Fair Rosamond literary treatment depends upon the priority of the version of William Warner or that of Samuel Daniel, both of which were published in 1592. The former poet, in his first edition (1586) of *Albion's England,* makes no mention of Rosamond, and in the second edition of 1589 he merely alludes to her: "The Kings fayre Leiman Rosamund, and how his Sonnes rebell/I overpasse;"[1] but in the third edition (1592) he gives one chapter to the story, which is allowed to stand with no significant change in the last edition of 1612.[2] Warner's edition of 1592 was not entered in the Stationers' Register, but Daniel's volume containing *The Complaint of Rosamond* was entered February 4, 1592, and was published before August of the same year.[3] Since in the preceding year Daniel had, according to his own statement, been "betraide by the indiscretion of a greedie Printer, and had some of [his] secrets bewraide to the world, uncorrected," and now was "forced to publish" the remainder of his sonnets,[4] it is not improbable that *The Complaint,* which he already had by him, was included to fill out the small volume. Warner's version could have been written at any time between late 1586 and 1592. Moreover, each poet appears to have fashioned his story independently of the other.[5] Indeed, Daniel seems unaware of any contemporary attempt to popularize the story, for Rosamond's ghost tells him that in him lies her one hope of a redemption of her fame:

> And were it not thy favourable lines
> Re-edified the wracke of my decayes,
> And that thy accents willingly assignes
> Some farther date, and give me longer daies,
> Few in this age had knowne my beauties praise.

[1] Bk. V, ch. xiiii, p. 104.

[2] 1592, bk. VIII, ch. xli, pp. 178-82; 1612, bk. VIII, ch. xli, pp. 198-201. I have used the 1612 edition.

[3] Thomas Nashe alludes to it in his *Pierce Penilesse* (McKerrow, I, 192), which was entered on August 8, 1592.

[4] Dedicatory epistle to Delia (1592). All quotations from *The Complaint* are from *The Complete Works in Verse and Prose of Samuel Daniel,* ed. Grosart, 5 vols. [London], 1885-96.

[5] See below, p. 18.

But thus renew'd, my fame redeemes some time,
Till other ages shall neglect thy Rime. (11.883-89)

Whereas Warner casts his story in the form of a versified *novella*, Daniel, apparently inspired by the success of Thomas Churchyard's *Jane Shore* (1563), uses the currently popular form of the medieval tragedy. There is, therefore, no convincing evidence for assigning priority to either version. Since, however, Warner's story is the simpler of the two, being not many more than one hundred fourteeners in length, and was not so immediately influential as Daniel's poem, we may first turn to it.

Warner omits from his story any reference to the casket, and makes only an allusion to the epitaph—"So died faire *Rose* (no longer Rose, nor faire, in sent, in sight)"—but he employs all the other ideas in sixteenth-century chronicle accounts and adds a number that are new. King Henry, already married to Eleanor of Aquitaine, disguises himself and wooes Rosamond as the king's agent.[6] Upon her refusal of his love he reveals his true identity and finally persuades her to become his mistress. He places her in a bower in the midst of a labyrinth at Woodstock, and provides her with maids and a "Knight of trust," who seeks to win her love but is repulsed. Eleanor and her three sons

[6] The idea of the king's wooing in disguise could very well have been derived by Warner from the "Shepherd's Tale" in Robert Greene's *Mourning Garment* (1590), although Warner later, in the Address "To the Reader" prefixed to his *Syrinx* (1597), apparently accuses Greene ("a Scholler better than my selfe, on whose grave the grasse now groweth green, whom otherwise, though otherwise to me guiltie, I name not") as one of the two writers who copied from him without acknowledgment. (See J. J. Jusserand, *The English Novel in the Time of Shakespeare* [London, 1890], p. 149.) Since Greene's story, though not of Rosamond Clifford, does bear some resemblance to hers, and may enter into the literary tradition through Warner and probably other writers, it may be briefly outlined here. Rosamond, the exceedingly beautiful daughter of the Thessalian shepherd Sydaris, fell in love with the shepherd swain Alexis. Soon news of the excellency of her beauty came to court, "where it was set out in such curious manner, and deciphered in such quaint phrases, that the king himselfe coveted to see her perfection; and therefore upon a day disguised himselfe, and went to the house of *Sydaris*, where, when he came, and saw the proportion of *Rosamond*, hee counted Fame partiall in her prattle, and man's tongue unable to discover that wherein the eye by viewing might surfet." The king fell in love with her and nobles at the court vied with one another for her hand, but all in vain, for still she loved Alexis. On the day appointed for her to choose publicly her mate, she chose Alexis. But Alexis meantime had married Phillida. Rosamond pined away and in a few days died, and Alexis, hearing of it, "went downe unto the water side, and in a fury hung himselfe upon a willow tree." The king erected a tomb and a monument to Rosamond's memory. (See *Works*, ed. Grosart, IX, 148-63.) The name Rosamond, the emphasis placed upon her great beauty, and the fact that she was wooed by a king in disguise who erected a monument to her—all these circumstances, being analogues to our story, made easy the incorporation of some of them into later versions of the story of Rosamond and Henry. See, for example, below, pp. 30-2.

regard Henry's infidelity with extreme disfavor, and, after many attempts to thread the labyrinth, she and her confederates at last succeed in overpowering the knight and in getting "the giding Clew" to the labyrinth. Confronted by the queen, Rosamond, whose exceeding beauty only increases the intruder's anger, falls to her knees, weeps, and begs for mercy.

> With that [the Queen] dasht her on the Lippes, so dyed double red:
> Then forc't she her to swallow downe (prepar'd for that intent)
> A poisoned Potion: which dispatcht, to whence they came they went.

Before she dies, Rosamond complains that beauty is a betrayer of those who possess it, concluding that "Vaine Beauty [should] stoupe to Vertue, for this latter is for ever." King Henry inters her body, puts his rebel sons to flight, and imprisons the queen, whom he never loves after.

It cannot be said that Warner had before him any one chronicle account of the story, but he strengthens all the hints he had found in such versions. He emphasizes Rosamond's beauty, and the baffling intricacy of the labyrinth, "built partly under ground:"

> Not *Sibils* Cave at *Cuma,* nor the Labyrinth in *Creat*
> Was like the Bower of *Rosamond,* for intricate and great.
> The Pellicane there neasts his Bird, and sporteth oft with her,
> Conducted by a Clew of thread, els could he not but err.

He closes his narrative with the king's interment of the body and his imprisonment of the queen, which Warner is the first writer to advance as her punishment for the murder of Rosamond. On the other hand, in order to make a complete story, the poet introduced many features which, though they are given in only the briefest form, become influential in the practice of many succeeding writers: the king's wooing Rosamond in disguise; his difficulty in winning her love; his providing her with maids and the trusty knight who unsuccessfully seeks to become a rival lover; the overpowering of the knight to get the clue to the labyrinth; the effect of Rosamond's beauty on Eleanor; the latter's brutal violence; Rosamond's plea for mercy in her helpless state, and her moralizing on beauty and virtue. Finally, it should be observed that the draught of poison as the cause of Rosamond's death appears in no version of the story before 1592.[7]

Daniel's poem of 130 rhyme-royal stanzas (including the twenty-three added in 1594, which in no wise contribute to the story) follows the convention of its type in having the ghost of his character tell her story to warn other maids by her tragic example. Denied passage to "the

[7] See below, p. 18, note 9.

sweet Elizian rest," Rosamond complains that she has been wronged by neglect, while "*Shores* wife is grac'd, and passes for a Saint" (l. 25)—an obvious allusion to the success of Churchyard's story—and asks the poet to tell her story "To teach to others what I learnt too late" (l. 67). Whereas Warner concerned himself chiefly with plot, Daniel's dignified poem is conceived on the highest level, artistic and moral; but the meager action and drama—our main concern here—though adequate for a story, constitute in reality no more than a framework for philosophical considerations and flights of poetic fancy.

The plot of Daniel's narrative may be outlined as follows: Rosamond lived quietly and unknown with her parents in the country until her friends, thinking her beauty "unfit for fields," sought to raise her honor by bringing her to the court (85-92). There King Henry fell in love with her. She successfully resisted his advances until "A seeming Matron, yet a sinfull Monster," added her persuasions (218ff.). She was then "train'd from Court,/T'a sollitarie Grange," and there the king visited her often, sent her daily messages, costly jewels, and "a Casket richly wrought" (372-413). Having seduced her,

> H'is driven to devise some subtill way,
> How he might safelyest keepe so rich a pray.
>
> A stately Pallace he forthwith did build,
> Whose intricate innumerable wayes
> With such confused errours, so beguilde
> Th' unguided Entrers, with uncertain strayes,
> And doubtfull turnings, kept them in delayes;
> With bootelesse labor leading them about,
> Able to find no way, nor in, nor out.
>
> Within the closed bosome of which frame,
> That serv'd a Centre to that goodly Round,
> Were lodgings, with a Garden to the same,
> With sweetest flowers that ev'r adorn'd the ground,
> And all the pleasures that delight hath found,
> T'entertaine the sense of wanton eies;
> Fuell of Love, from whence lusts flames arise.
>
> . . . .
>
> None but the King might come into the place,
> With certain Maides that did attend my neede,
> And he himselfe came guided by a threed. (468-90)

Gossip carried the news to the ears of the queen, and, fired with jealousy but waiting until the king was absent, she entered the labyrinth by

> that Threed,
> That serv'd a conduct to my absent Lord,
> Left there by chance (582-4),

and forced Rosamond to take poison (597ff., 771ff.). The king came upon her body as it was being conveyed to the funeral, and, after many outpourings of shock, grief, and love over his dead Rose, he swore vengeance (778-856), promised to honor her in monuments to her memory, and interred her body "in honorable wise" at Godstow,

> Where yet as now scarce any note descries
> Unto these times, the memory of me,
> Marble and Brasse so little lasting be. (871-5)

The simple materials with which Daniel constructs his plot are obviously derived from chronicle accounts, both early and late. Although he makes only a faint allusion to Rosamond's epitaph (l. 861), he puts the account of the casket to clever artistic use by substituting for the marvellous giants, beasts, fowls, and fishes of Higden the classical stories of Amymone and Neptune and of Io and Jove, with appropriate comments by Rosamond herself. He is almost as sparing of detail in his description of the labyrinth as the chroniclers were, and he follows the later ones in using a clue of thread and in declining to elaborate on the difficulties Queen Eleanor encountered in reaching Rosamond's lodging. There is some reason, also, to think that he had made use of *The French Chronicle of London,* or a similar account, in his detailing of the events following Rosamond's death. The king's coming upon her body as it was being taken to Godstow for interment; his outbursts of amazement and grief; his shows of affection;[8] his swearing of vengeance, together with his promise to perpetuate her memory—all these are to be found in no earlier version except *The French Chronicle.*

Resemblances of Daniel's version to Warner's, save for the moralizing on beauty and virtue, which, after all, could well have been suggested by the very nature of the theme, may all be accounted for by a common source in the chronicles. Differences are such as to suggest that neither version was in any way dependent on the other. In the present state of our knowledge, Daniel must vie with Warner for the honor of being the first creative writer to assign poisoning at the hands of Queen Eleanor as the cause of Rosamond's death.[9]

[8] The passage I have in mind (ll. 792-847, especially ll. 840-7), which has often been brought into comparison with that in *Romeo and Juliet* (V, iii, 92ff.), could have been inspired by Henry's outburst in the *Chronicle* (see above, p. 10).

[9] Stow, in his *Annales* (1592), p. 219, is the only chronicler to specify the nature of Rosamond's death: she was "poysoned by Q. Elianor as some thought." But since his Preface is dated May 26, 1592, and Daniel's *Complaint* had been entered

Finally, Daniel did contribute at least three new features to the story which were used by later writers in one form or another. I refer to the matron whose persuasions help to weaken Rosamond's resistance to the king's advances, the use of the love-pictures on the casket for the same purpose, and the solitary grange as a place of assignation and seduction of Rosamond prior to her seclusion in the labyrinth.

The impression made by Daniel's poem was immediate and lasting, and it was his story, with others written under its influence, which demonstrated to the better craftsmen the possibilities of the Rosamond theme for literary treatment. Thomas Nashe, who in the preceding year had had some part in the surreptitious publication of some of Daniel's sonnets, singled out *The Complaint* as a "rare Poem" characterized by "exquisite paines and puritie of witte,"[10] and in 1593, when Thomas Churchyard brought out his "beautified . . . Shores wife" to prove his aged wits were still "ripe and reddie," he complimented Daniel in both word and deed.[11] In his high praise for the "new

---

in the Stationers' Register on the preceding February 4th, priority may be assigned to Daniel. The actual source of the idea cannot be established with certainty, but it seems likely that in its slow development the story of Fair Rosamond was at some time, and maybe at many times, confused with that of sixth-century Rosamunda, queen of the Lombards, first told by Paulus Diaconus (*Historia Langobardum,* lib. i, 27, and li, 28-30), and retold by many others, among them Higden in his *Polychronicon* (see above, p. 8), Gower in his *Confessio Amantis* (lib. i, 2459-2646), Machiavelli in his *Florentine History* (tr. by T. B., Esquire [London, 1595], pp. 6-7), and George Turberville as "the fift historie" of *Tragicall Tales* (1587); and later used by Thomas Middleton in *The Witch.* The similarity of the names Rosamond and Rosamunda, the identity of the epitaphs assigned to them (see above, p. 8), and the presence in both stories of intrigue, jealousy, revenge, treachery, and, finally, death by poison—all point to the plausibility of such a confusion.

[10] *Pierce Penilesse,* in *Works,* ed. McKerrow, 5 vols. (London, 1910), I, 192.

[11] *Churchyards Challenge* (London, 1593), Dedication, p. 126. The association of the names of Rosamond and Jane Shore in literary practice and comment, first suggested by Daniel (*Complaint,* 1. 25), continues even as late as the nineteenth century, when chapbooks often print the two stories together or refer in one to the other (see below, pp. 44, 45, 48). See, for example, Giles Fletcher, "Rising to the Crowne of Richard the Third" (1593), in Arber's *English Garner,* VIII, 465; John Willoughbie, *Willoughbie His Avisa* (1594), ed. G. B. Harrison (London, 1926), p. 34; Thomas Campion, *Elegiarum Liber* (1595), in *Works,* ed. Vivian (Oxford, 1909), p. 338. Deloney's ballads on Rosamond and Shore's wife, which may have been written as early as 1593, are placed together at the beginning of *The Garland of Good Will* (ed. of 1631); Drayton, in *England's Heroical Epistles* (1597), gives each mistress an exchange of epistles with her lover. *A New Ballad of King Edward and Jane Shore* (rep. in *Roxb. Ballads,* VIII, 423-44) refers to Rosamond. See also *The Fruits of Jealousie; or, A Love (but not Loving) Letter* (1615), p. 86, in *The Blazon of Jealousie,* tr. R. T. [ofte] (London, 1615), Sig. N3^v; *The Woful Lamentation of Mrs. Jane Shore,* in *Roxb. Ballads,* I, 162-3 (cf. *ibid.,* I, 184); John Gay, *Shepherd's Week* (1714), ed. Faber (London, 1926), VI, 119; *History of Jane Shore* (Newcastle, *n. d.*), pp. 23-4; *The Unfortunate Royal Mistresses* (London, *n.d.*), a miscellany of works on both characters.

shepheard late up sprong," Spenser forecasts that Daniel's true vein will be "In Tragick plaints and passionate mischance."[12] In 1598, Francis Meres comments that "every one passionateth when he readeth the afflicted death of Daniel's distressed Rosamond."[13] Similar is Phineas Fletcher's reference to the effectiveness of the story of Rosamond,

> Whom late a shepherd taught to weep so sore,
> That woods and hardest rocks her harder fate deplore.[14]

The Complaint not only prompted Churchyard's recension of *Shores Wife* (1593) but became the common inspiration of a whole group of poems: Anthony Chute's *Beawtie Dishonoured* (1593), Thomas Lodge's *Elstred* (1593), probably Giles Fletcher's *Rising to the Crowne of Richard III* (published with his *Licia* in 1593), Drayton's *Piers Gaveston* (1594?) and *Matilda* (1594).

In the last poem, Drayton expresses his admiration for Daniel's poem, "Recorded in the lasting Book of Fame,"[15] and three years later opened his *England's Heroical Epistles,* dedicated to Lucy, Countess of Bedford, with "The Epistle of Rosamond to King Henry the Second."[16] The letter form adopted by Drayton, for which he derived only a suggestion from the *Heroides* of Ovid, afforded him the advantage of being able to set forth directly the thoughts and emotions of his characters—though Daniel's use of Rosamond's ghost as his mouthpiece did much the same thing for her, yet not for Henry. The letter form enabled Drayton to deal convincingly with the present, but confined him to random reminiscence of the past. The most serious limitation which it imposed, however, was that it made any plot in the usual sense impossible, and precluded his completion of the tragedy. On the other hand, perhaps any loss suffered in these respects is more than compensated by the intimate insight which the reader acquires into two characters involved in an intensified dramatic situation. This welcome achievement would in some degree explain the sudden and

[12] *C. C. C. H. A.*, 11. 416-26.

[13] *Elizabethan Critical Essays,* ed. G. Gregory Smith, 2 vols. (Oxford, 1904), II, 316.

[14] *Purple Island,* V. 45, in *Works,* ed. F. S. Boas, 2 vols. (Cambridge, 1909), II, 63.

[15] *Works,* ed. Hebel, I, 214.

[16] In the Dedication, which is devoted wholly to the letters of Rosamond and Henry, he writes as if many literary works on the subject had preceded his: "Madam, after all the admired wits of this excellent age, which have laboured in the sad complaints of faire and unfortunate *Rosamond,* and by the excellence of invention, have sounded the depth of her sundry passions," etc. (1597 ed.) Only Warner, Daniel, and, possibly, Deloney had dealt creatively with the theme.

continued popularity of the *Epistles* in an age that had become habituated to witnessing and reading dramatic representations.

To King Henry in France, a lonely and remorseful Rosamond, immured in the great labyrinth at Woodstock,[17] writes that every sight and activity of her daily rounds serves only to remind her of her degredation and woe. She asks him to rid her of her shame by taking her life:

> My Life's a Blemish, which doth cloud thy Name,
> Take it away, and cleare shall shine thy Fame:
> Yeeld to my Sute, if ever Pittie mov'd thee,
> In this shew Mercie, as I ever lov'd thee.[18]

To her Henry replies that he has his troubles, too—no man more—and Fortune has bereft him of all comfort save his love. He seeks to alleviate her sense of shame by reinterpreting her reminders of it. Not without foreboding of ill to come, he ardently declares his supreme love of her:

> Accursed be that Heart, that Tongue, that Breath,
> Should thinke, should speake, or whisper of thy Death;
> For in one Smile, or Lowre from thy sweet Eye,
> Consists my Life, my Hope, my Victorie. (199-202)

Drayton's conception of Rosamond is derived from Daniel, but the character of Henry, which is well drawn, is his own. His conception of the story itself must be pieced together from references here and there. From Daniel he took over the "wicked Woman," who had Rosamond "taste the Fruit of Good and Evill," and so corresponds in office to Daniel's "seeming Matron, yet a sinfull Monster." From the same poet he derived the casket, with its representations of Amymone and Neptune and Io and Jove.[19] Vaughan, the only other person who knew the secret ways of the labyrinth, and who, according to Drayton's note, was "a Knight, whom the King exceedingly loved, who kept the Palace at *Woodstock*, and much of the Kings Jewels and Treasure, to whom the King committed many of his Secrets, and in whom he reposed such trust, that he durst commit his Love unto his Charge" (p. 146), was no doubt suggested by the "Knight of trust" who attended Rosamond in Warner's poem, and from whom the clue was taken by force. Although his poems are meritorious in artistic conception and execution, Drayton really adds nothing to the plot of the story.

[17] For Drayton's description of the labyrinth, see above, p. 7.
[18] *Works*, ed. Hebel. Vol. II, p. 138, 11. 191-4.
[19] For minor similarities to Daniel, see Hebel, V, 102-3.

The most frequently reprinted of the early versions of the Rosamond story is the ballad beginning "Whenas King *Henry* rul'd this land, the second of that name," attributed to Thomas Deloney and written probably before March of 1593,[20] probably printed in the now lost edition of *The Garland of Good Will* issued in the same year, and actually in *Strange Histories* in 1607. Its popularity is attested by the many reprintings of it and by its use in versions of the Rosamond story as late as the nineteenth century.[21] It is evident that the main source of Deloney's version is William Warner's story in his *Albion's England:* the "Knight of trust," who was Rosamond's keeper in Warner, becomes "a valiant Knight" named Sir Thomas (33-6, 121-4); entrance to the bower is gained by overpowering Sir Thomas and getting from him the "clew of twined thred" (137-42); the queen is amazed at Rosamond's beauty and attire (145-50); on her knees, Rosamond makes a tearful plea for mercy and pardon (153-72); she drinks poison and is entombed "at Godstow, neere to *Oxford* Towne as may be seene this day" (183-92). Noteworthy rejections from Warner's version are the wooing by the king in disguise, the knight as would-be rival lover, and the punishment of Eleanor by imprisonment. Deloney adds the details that the labyrinth was built "of stone and timber strong" and had "An hundred and fifty doores." Moreover, an entirely new feature of the story is Rosamond's request that she may accompany the king to France as his page:

> Nay rather let me, like a Page,
> your shield and Target beare,
> That on my brest the blow may light,
> that should annoy you there. (93-6)[22]

Deloney's Rosamond shows no shame, and he stresses her youth and beauty, and her unreserved love of Henry. In her plea to the queen

[20] For a discussion of the date of the ballad and a list of the various editions of anthologies in which it appeared, see F. O. Mann's ed. of *The Works of Thomas Deloney* (Oxford, 1912), pp. 562-64; 585.

[21] John Aubrey says his nurse sang it to him (see Thoms's *Anecdotes,* Camden Soc., V, 104-5). See Percy's *Reliques,* ed. Wheatley (London, 1910), II, 158ff.; Ritson's *Ancient Songs and Ballads,* 2 vols. (London, 1829), II, 120-7; Percy Society, XV (1845), ii. 12; XXX (1852), 1-9; Child's *English and Scottish Popular Ballads,* VII (London, 1861), 283-91; *Roxburghe Ballads,* ed. Ebsworth, VI (1889), 667-75; and eighteenth- and nineteenth-century reprints listed in *B. M. Cat. of Printed Books* under "The Life and Death of Rosamond," etc. For an eighteenth-century ballad on the same subject by another hand, see below, pp. 31-2.

[22] Queen Eleanor once attempted to escape to France disguised in male attire. See Agnes Strickland, *Lives of the Queens of England,* 8 vols. (Philadelphia, 1893), I, 280. Could this incident have been transferred by oral tradition to Rosamond and resulted in her plea to accompany King Henry to France as his page?

for mercy, she asks pardon for her offences, as in Warner, but, unlike his Rosamond, she entreats the queen's pity on her youthful years and offers to renounce her sinful life and live in a cloister or suffer banishment if only her life may be spared (155-68). Deloney's striking dependence upon Warner rather than upon Daniel may be explained by the fact that as a ballad-writer he was primarily interested in plot, and for plot-suggestions Warner had much to offer.

As a sequel to the Rosamond story, Deloney wrote a ballad called "The Imprisonment of Queene Elenor," first printed in *Strange Histories* in 1602. Based on the account given in Holinshed (1587 ed., II, 117) of the queen's release by her son King Richard from sixteen years' imprisonment, it gives prominence to her confession of the poisoning of "Sweete Rosamond that was so faire."[23] The four extant editions of the collection (1602, 1607, 1670? and 1674) made this story so well known in the seventeenth century that out of it grew another widely-known ballad, "Queen Eleanor's Confession" (*c* 1685), in which the queen is represented as confessing the poisoning of Rosamond to the king and the earl marshal disguised as friars.[24]

A variation on the commonly-assigned manner of Rosamond's death must be noticed here, for it suggests both a reaction to the mystification of that circumstance as reported by the chroniclers, and a breaking-up of the pattern established by Warner, Daniel, and Deloney. It appears in *A Pleasant Commodie, Called Look about You* (1600), in which the action centers about the settlement of the difficulties between King Henry and his rebellious sons. The leading comic character, one Skinke, who has "poysoned red cheekt *Rosamond*" at the bidding of Queen Eleanor and with the approval of young King Henry, is promised pardon by the young King Richard and Earl John. The Earl of Leicester argues that Queen Eleanor, who, so all the world thinks, was imprisoned because of her "pitty and affection to her sonne" (whose rebellion she abetted), in reality

> Is kept close prisoner for an acte of Justice,
> Committed on an odious Concubine.[25]

[23] See *Works,* ed. Mann, pp. 397-99. In the same collection of *Strange Histories* Deloney further shows his interest in the events of King Henry's reign in the ballad, "How King *Henry* the second crowning his Sonne king of *England,* in his owne lifetime, was by him most grievously vexed with warres," etc.

[24] See Percy's *Reliques*, ed. Wheatley, II, 164ff.; Percy Soc., II (London, 1823), 327ff.; Roxb. Ballads, VI, 680-1; Child, 5 vols. (Boston and New York [1882-98]), III, 258-64; IV, 498-9. Child gives seven versions of the ballad, in five of which Rosamond's murder is numbered among the sins of Queen Eleanor. For early versions and analogues in which a husband, disguised as a shrift-father, hears his wife's confession, see Child, III, 256-8.

[25] Malone Soc. Rep. (Oxford, 1913), ll. 114-36.

Lancaster replies that true it is that Rosamond sinned, but that Eleanor, the "bellowes of seditious fine," has committed a greater sin in arming her sons against their father (148-70). If, as has been said, this episode in the play is a significant reflection of current thinking about the story of Rosamond and possibly of a desire to expand it, it may be pointed out that the shifting of the act of poisoning from Queen Eleanor to a low character who serves as her agent opened up new possibilities for later writers which they were quick to use to advantage. It may be added, also, that the debate between Leicester and Lancaster foreshadows not only the villainous character assigned by later writers to the Earl of Leicester, but indicates a clash between the historical fact that Eleanor was imprisoned for abetting rebellion and the belief generated by oral, and later by literary, tradition that the crime for which she was punished was the murder of Fair Rosamond.

This variance between history and the oral or literary tradition is a consideration of some interest in the study of the development of a literary work which may draw from both. Every author since the seventeenth century who has dealt at length with the story of Rosamond has had to cope with the problem of making adjustments between the claims of the two. It is noteworthy that Samuel Daniel, who a generation before had done so much to popularize the story, omits any reference to it in his popular *Collection of the Historie of England* (1618, 1621, 1626, 1634). More surprising, in view of the scope and nature of his work, is Thomas Heywood's failure to make any use of it in his *Nine Bookes of Various History, concerninge Women, Inscribed by the Names of the Nine Muses* (1624).[26] Among historians in verse the attitude is often different. Thomas Slatyer (or Slater), in his tumbling-verse *History of Great Britaine* (1621), because of the ambitious breadth of his subject, has but a bare sketch of the story; but he accepts the labyrinth and "bowers" at Woodstock, the poisoning of Rosamond, during the king's absence in France, by the furious and jealous queen, and the latter's imprisonment for this and the incitement of her rebellious sons.[27] Slatyer gives but some fifteen lines to the story, and makes no attempt to embroider it. Thomas May, however, devotes to the legend considerable portions of three of the seven books which make up his *Reigne of King Henry the Second* (1633), written "by his Majesties Command."[28]

May's attitude toward the comparative heinousness of the sins of the two female offenders may be inferred from Rosamond's dying speech to Eleanor:

[26] But see Fuller and others below, p. 28ff.

[27] London, 1621, p. 241.

[28] For general information about the poem, see A. G. Chester, *Thomas May: Man of Letters* (Philadelphia, 1932). Chester has indicated no specific borrowings or influences in the poem.

If you had spar'd my life, I might have beene
In time to come th' example of your glory;
Not of your shame, as now. for when the story
Of haplesse *Rosamund* is read; the best
And holyest people, as they will detest
My crime, and call it foule: they will abhorre
And call unjust the rage of *Elianor*.
And in this act of yours it will be thought
Hing [*sic*] *Henry's* sorrow, not his love you sought.[29]

The story, which is interwoven among other events of Henry's reign and decorated with somewhat elaborate mythological passages, is as follows: At the great festival following the coronation of Henry's son at Westminster, among the great beauties in attendance appears Fair Rosamond, with whom Henry instantly falls desperately in love. After the festivities she returns to the country, and Henry is called to France. During his absence from England, she is brought up to court "to waite on *Elianor* the Queene." Upon his return he strives secretly to impress Rosamond, in spite "of *Elianor*, and her officious spies." She feels flattered by his many attentions, but she does not love him. Thinking to avoid the dangers of wooing her at court, Henry lodges her in "A faire retreat of greater privacy/Removed from London" . . .

No farther distance then, at ease, a day
Might reach from London, stood the place, which they
Had chose for beautious *Rosamund* to bide,
Within a forrest, rarely beautify'd
Without, by all that nature could afford;
Within the house it selfe was richly stor'd
(As guesse you may) with what a bounteous King
To please his dearest Mistres eye would bring.
The place it selfe did seeme his sute to move,
And intimate a silent plea for love.

. . . .

About this house such groves, springs, gardens were,
As Poëts placed in Loves region, where
The Westwinds ever blow, faire youth doth stay,
And keepes from thence old age and care away. (E2-E3)

There she was attended by "An ancient Dame skill'd in those arts" . . .

To aide the kings desires; of most profound
And subtle wit, of winning speech was she;
And such in all, she might be thought to bee
No Beldame, but wise *Venus* lurking in
A Beldames shape, faire *Rosamund* to winne. (E2v.)

[29] London, 1633, sig. I 7v.-8r.

By showing Rosamond salacious pictures in the gallery and by offering cunning arguments, this Dame so prevailed over her that Henry was able to seduce her (E3-5). Later he was again called to France, but before he left

> A sumptuous bower did he at Woodstock build,
> Whose structure by *Daedalian* art was fill'd
> With winding Mazes, and perplexed wayes;
> Which who so enters, still deceived strayes
> Unlesse by guidance of a clew of thread
> Through those obscure Maeanders he be led.
> There with all objects that delight might lend,
> And with such chosen servants to attend
> And guard her, as had still beene faithfull knowne,
> Dooes *Henry* leave this beautious Paragon. (E6r.)

During his absence,

> Pale *Nemesis* that had possest before
> The jealous brest of raging *Elianor,*
> In far more horrid shapes was enter'd now,
> And all her wrongs in doubled formes did show;
> 'Mongst which (the deepest piercing wrong) she found
> Her bed despis'd for love of *Rosamund.*
> Then madd she raves; tis not the subtilty
> Of that *Daedalian* Labyrinth (quoth she)
> Shall hide the strumpet from my vengeful hand;
> Nor can her doating champion *Henry* stand
> Against me now to guard his Paramour.
> If through the winding Mazes of her bower
> No art nor skill can passe: the World shall know
> A Queenes revenge; the house Ile overthrow,
> Levell those lustfull buildings with the ground,
> And in their ruines tombe his *Rosamund.* (I 3-4)

To carry out her purpose, she moved to Oxford, and every day lurked near Woodstock "to descry/A Way to act this baleful tragedy." Rosamond, sitting alone one day in her chamber, is horrified by the cry of her maid, from whom the queen had taken the clue. Eleanor and her attendants enter, but at the sight of Rosamond's beauty they almost falter in their design. Rosamond, commanded by the queen to drink poison, and finding that reason and a plea for time are of no avail, drinks from the cup, asks pardon for herself, for Henry, even for the queen, and dies. They bury her at Godstow Abbey, and when Henry returns from abroad, Queen Eleanor, for this act and for her part in abetting the rebellion of her sons, is by the king's order imprisoned for the rest of his reign. (I 4v.-8v.)

Although May's narrative of Henry and Rosamond is woven into other events of Henry's busy reign, such as his wars abroad and at home and his conflict with Becket leading to martyrdom, it is evident that the author had in mind a definite design for the whole action. Despite the fact that the story itself is greatly expanded by long descriptive and mythological passages,[30] the plot is simple, being derived from Daniel's *Complaint of Rosamond,* with only a few alterations of minor importance. The meeting at the coronation festival is more specific and plausible than Daniel's brief and vague treatment of the encounter of the two lovers at court. Daniel's "seeming Matron" becomes May's "ancient Dame," procuresses both; the place of seduction, the "solitarie Grange" of Daniel, is expanded into the "faire retreat," but made much more pretentious and rich; the love stories which appear on the casket in Daniel's poem are elaborated into an entire picture gallery, and are used for the same purpose of weakening Rosamond's resistance; and May's description of the bower follows Daniel's closely. On the other hand, May makes much more of the initial stages of the love-passion, emphasizing Rosamond's resistance, and logically enough, he elaborates the wiles of the procuress. He is, however, original in having Eleanor take the clue of thread from the hand of Rosamond's maid. The effect of Rosamond's beauty on the queen and her confederates, it is true, reminds one rather of Warner and Deloney, and it should be noted, moreover, that May provides for the punishment of Eleanor, a matter which we find only in Warner among earlier poets.

When Thomas May's poem appeared in 1633, the story of Fair Rosamand had already established a place for itself in literary tradition. Warner, Daniel, Drayton, Deloney, and May had all dealt with the theme in narrative verse, and each author had employed a different type of poem as his medium; Warner, the simple and brief tale; Daniel, the conventional and popular medieval tragedy; Drayton, the epistolary exchange; Deloney, the ballad; and May, the historical romance. It is a no less puzzling than curious fact that in an age when almost every conceivable kind of matter was thought fit for representation on the stage, the Rosamond story (except for a brief fragment of it in *Look about You*) never became the subject of a play.[31] A full century was to pass, after the appearance of the versions of Warner and Daniel, before it was cast in dramatic form; but it was on the stage in the eighteenth and nineteenth centuries that it was destined to achieve its greatest popularity. Strange as this belated development may seem, it is even

[30] Such as making Pallas, in the Homeric manner, appear to Henry in a vision in which he sees the future rulers of England and is made to appreciate the true greatness of those distant successors bearing the names of James and Charles (D4-6).

[31] But see below, p. 69, note 1.

more difficult to explain why it was that, once the theme had attained such early success and popularity in the various types of narrative poem, no writer of distinction made any noteworthy use of it in that form until John Masefield wrote his *Rose of the World* (1931). May it be said that, once it had proved itself an attractive story for dramatic treatment and for chapbook and historical novel, no competent literary craftsman cared to offer the mild form of a narrative poem in competition?

This is not to say that either readers or writers ignored the story for a time after its initial success. There is reason to think that quite the contrary was true, for in those early years Rosamond as an English beauty had not only surpassed in fame the celebrated Jane Shore, of whose popularity Daniel makes her ghost envious, but to at least one poet, whose English pride may very well have been representative, she had come to mean to England what Helen of Troy had meant to the ancients. To illustrate that beauty is not bound to one age or clime, Thomas Campion declares,

> *Hellen,* I grant, might pleasing be;
> And *Ros'mond* was as sweet as shee.[32]

Quoting Daniel and Drayton, Robert Burton used her name and story to illustrate the fury of jealousy in woman and the power of feminine beauty to overcome even the greatest of men.[33] Phineas Fletcher even uses the Daedalian work of Rosamond's labyrinth to elucidate the intricacy of the aural passages![34] At least two admirers of Drayton's poems helped to perpetuate Rosamond's fame. In 1653, Nicholas Hookes, in his *Miscellanea Poetica,* appended to his *Amanda, a Sacrifice to an Unknown Goddess,* prints Drayton's exchange of epistles by Rosamond and Henry together with Latin translations of them;[35] and John Oldmixon included in his *Amores Britannici* (1703) the same exchange, which "despite the author's claims to independence amounts to a literal translation from Elizabethan to Augustan English."[36]

Among other significant sidelights on the history of the theme is the interest of the antiquaries. In view of the greatly increased activity in the study of history and antiquities in the seventeenth century, it is not surprising to learn that searchers of the antique springs who had fallen

[32] *Works,* ed. Vivian (Oxford, 1909), p. 136.

[33] *Anatomy of Melancholy,* ed. Shilleto, 3 vols. (London, 1923), III, 77-8, 87, 93-4, 324, 587ff.

[34] *Purple Island,* V, 45, in *Works,* ed. Boas, 2 vols. (Cambridge, 1909), II, 62-3.

[35] London, 1653, pp. 164-91.

[36] J. W. Hebel in *Works of Michael Drayton,* V, 97. For a less dependent imitation of Drayton, see William Pattison and *Fair Rosamond to the Fair Hibernian* (1757), below, pp. 32-3.

under the spell of Fair Rosamond were displaying a sometimes eager romantic interest in everything associated with her name. Although Thomas Fuller reveals no marked enthusiasm for the legend, he does give Rosamond a place among the "memorable persons" of Herefordshire, and mentions the labyrinth at Woodstock and Queen Eleanor's murder of her.[37] From certain passages in Anthony à Wood's *Life* one may infer that he had given more than passing attention to the storied places that whispered her name—an interest, I might add, that prepared the way for local poems on Woodstock in the next century. Commenting on the market near Woodstock, he says that it was permitted to be kept on the Lord's day because King Henry so "much delighted in that place for ye sake of his beloved Rosamond," and he tells of a walk he had with Sr Tanner of All Souls to Godstow, "where I told him the antiquities of that place, so eat a dish of fish, and went through part of Wolvercote home."[38] Another antiquary, Thomas Hearne, had such a passion for the subject that to the editors of Dugdales' *Monasticon*[39] he "seems entirely to have lost his discrimination as an antiquary when dilating upon the history of Rosamond."[40] Apparently, he returned to the romantic associations of the story over a number of years, and often visited Woodstock to view and speculate upon the ruins of the great palace there.[41]

The repeated interest of such antiquaries helps us to understand the attraction which Woodstock held for other writers of less specialized points of view in the eighteenth century. The author of *Windsor Forest,* for example, must be numbered among the pilgrims to Fair Rosamond's shrine. "We paid a visit to the spring where Rosamond bathed herself," he writes to an anonymous correspondent; "on a hill, where remains only a piece of a wall of the old palace of Henry II. We toasted her shade in cold water, not without a thought or two, scarce so cold as the liquor we drank it in."[42] Pope's visit did not result in a local poem, but other poets of his time found in Rosamond's supposed place of residence a subject for the kind of poem in which

[37] *Worthies,* ed. P. Austin Nuttall, 3 vols. (London, 1840), II, 82.

[38] *Athenae Oxon.,* ed. Bliss, I, lxxx, cxxii.

[39] Caley, Ellis, and Bardinel, 6 vols. (London, 1817-30), IV, 358.

[40] For the facts and speculations which Hearne published, see his appendixes to his editions of William of Newburgh's *Historia Rerum Anglicarum* (1719) and John Leland's *Itinerary* (1710-12), II.

[41] See *Reliquiae Hearnaniae,* ed. Philip Bliss (Oxford, 1857), pp. 97-8; 374: "We viewed the old ruins about Rosamund's well in Woodstocke park. There are the ruins of the labyrinth for Rosamund. This labyrinth was a vast thing;" p. 423: "This day I walked to Woodstock, and took a fresh view of the old foundations of Rosamund's bower, which are just by her poole."

[42] *Works of Alexander Pope,* ed. Elwin and Courthope, 10 vols. (London, 1871-89) X, 265.

Pope achieved success. In *Woodstock Park,* published in 1706, William Harrison briefly relates "Great Henry's Flame, and Rosamunda's Fate." Though the story is not told, the poet's fancy recalls Rosamond's beauty, the wondrous bower, and Eleanor's jealous fury. Thomas Tickell, who had already paid his tribute in verse to Addison's *Rosamond,*[43] turns his attention to Woodstock in his poem *On the Prospect of Peace* (1712) as a place

> Where kings of old, conceal'd, forgot the throne,
> And beauty was content to shine unknown;
> Where love and war by turns pavilions rear,
> And Henry's bowers near Blenheim's dome appear;
> And weary'd champion lull in soft alcoves,
> The noblest boast of thy romantic groves.
> Oft, if the Muse presage, shall he be seen
> By Rosamonda fleeting o'er the green,
> In dreams be hail'd by heroes' mighty shades.[44]

In 1759 John Gilbert Cooper wrote a poem, published in 1762 as *Woodstock: an Elegy,*[45] in which the poet, wandering along "winding Isis' willowed bank," and deploring the "varying scenes of fortune," sees the "gloomy mansion" which contains the vault of Fair Rosamond. A ghost appears and laments that time cannot destroy remembrance of her love and fate. The poet is then transported to "the summit of a cloud-built height" whence he sees a labyrinth rising out of the ground "to sounds of melting note"—an intricate maze with a grotto in the center. On the bank of a stream

> A Beauty lay, surpassing all the train
> Of Virgin Delia, or Idalia's queen.

By her lies a form imperial garlanded with roses and myrtle. Little loves flutter on the boughs. As King Henry, now sated with love, leaves, Queen Eleanor appears with a pointed dagger and a poisoned bowl. "Ah, stop, inhuman," cries the poet, and then with a thunderclap the vision disappears.

But we now turn from the trite and artificial flights of Cooper's local poem, which represents little more than a bad fashion in writing and contributes nothing to the development of Rosamond's story. In the age when these effusions were being written, the popular poet, the

[43] Printed in Addison's *Poetical Miscellanies: the Sixth Part* in 1709 and later prefixed to the third edition of his *Rosamond* (1713). See below, pp. 72ff.

[44] *Works of the English Poets,* ed. Samuel Johnson, XXIX (1790), 164-5.

[45] Reprinted in *A Collection of Poems,* 2 vols. (London, 1768), II, 155-67, and in *Bell's Classical Arrangement of Fugitive Poetry,* IX (1789), 9-21, and reviewed in *The Monthly Review,* XXV (1762), 62-4.

maker of ballads, was also at work. *The Unfortunate Concubine; or, Rosamond's Overthrow,* "occasioned," as the rest of the title informs us, "by her Brother's praising her beauty to two young knights of Salisbury, as they rid along the Road," first appeared in 1723 in J. Roberts' *Collection of Old Ballads* (I, 4), and, in the judgment of Ebsworth,[46] dates not much earlier than that year, though I am inclined to place it much earlier.[47] It possesses many of the characteristics of the folk ballad, and I can discover no hint of its dependence on any literary versions, unless, as I doubt, it may derive from the earliest known chapbook, *The Life and Death of Fair Rosamond* (c. 1640), though it could be argued as well that it antedates the chapbook. But first let us turn to the tale which the ballad tells.

Young Clifford, so the story goes, riding along a road in the vicinity of Oxford with two other young knights of Salisbury, boasts of the peerless beauty of his sister Rosamond. His praises of her are heard by King Henry, who is in a bower nearby, and the king resolves to have her. He commands young Clifford to carry "three letters seal'd with gold" to his sister, and the knight reluctantly obeys. Upon reading the letters, Rosamond, overcome with fear, curses her brother for his boasting, calls for her "planet-book," and discovers that she is to die of poisoning. She obeys the king's command, however, moves to court, and becomes his mistress. Report of the king's new concubine enrages the queen, and after great difficulty she finds the clue to Rosamond's bower where the king kept her, and, deaf to her rival's pleas for mercy, compels her to drink the fatal cup. The king, infuriated and heartbroken at the news of the queen's vile deed, casts her in prison, "where she lay six and twenty years" until after Henry's death, her son set her free.

> And she set many more at large,
> Who long for debt had lain;
> Her royal pity did discharge
> Thousands in Richard's reign.[48]

One matter of interest in this version of the story is that those elements which are traditional—Rosamond's becoming the king's mistress, the jealous queen's reaching her by a clue, and the circumstances of the poisoning—are vague, as if derived from an oral version from

[46] *Roxb. Ballads*, VI, p. 672. The ballad is printed in VI, 676-8. It is printed also in *Old Ballads Historical and Narrative*, 4 vols. (London, 1810), II, 68-77, and in *The Unfortunate Royal Mistresses* (London, n. d.), pp. 34-40.

[47] See below, pp. 41-2.

[48] Cf. Holinshed's *Chronicles* (1587), II, 117. This enlargement of prisoners is used also in Deloney's "Imprisonment of Queen *Elenor*." See Works, ed. Mann, p. 399.

which details had dropped out either because they were not recalled or were regarded as unnecessary for an audience well acquainted with them. There is, moreover, no reference to a labyrinth, and there is no provision for Rosamond's burial at Godstow. On the other hand, we discover at the same time some elements alien to the tradition. The device by which Rosamond's beauty is brought to the king's attention —by the praise of a relative—is to be found only in "The Shepherd's Tale" of Robert Greene's *Mourning Garment*, which has to do with a different Rosamond.[49] But nothing remotely similar to the "three letters seal'd with gold" and Rosamond's "planet-book" which foretells her death by poisoning, had appeared in any recorded version of the story. These circumstances, together with at least a score of images in the ballad which suggest a communal origin, invite the belief that the ballad is much older than its date of publication. Its opening incident, we shall see, becomes a popular device in later versions of the story.

In 1728 appeared two poetical epistles, an exchange between Rosamond and Henry, written by William Pattison in the manner of Michael Drayton.[50] In her epistle to King Henry, Rosamond recalls memories of their past love, and regrets, in the manner of Daniel, that she had ever left the country for the court:

> Oh! had I liv'd in some obscure retreat,
> Securely fair, and innocently sweet;
> How had I bless'd some humble shepherd's arms!
> How kept my fame as spotless as my charms!
> Then hadst thou ne'er beheld these eyes of mine,
> Nor they bewail'd the fatal power of thine!

and, like Drayton's Rosamond, finds that everything about her serves only to recall her happier days spent on the manor in Henry's company. She relates, among other things, a dream she had had, warning her of her fate:

> Embosom'd in a vale, thou know'st the shade,
> Fast by the murmurs of a soft cascade:
> There, while one night full beams of Cynthia play,
> (Warm was the night) with wanderings tir'd, I lay
> Till, by degrees, the falling waters clos'd
> My eye-lids, and my wearied limbs repos'd.
> Sudden the fairy Monarch I behold,
> Near he approach'd, and thus my fate foretold:

[49] See above, p. 15, note 6. But cf. the early chapbook version below, pp. 40ff.

[50] Reprinted in *A Classical Arrangement of Fugitive Poetry*, VII (London, 1797), 1-15, and in *The Poetical Calendar*, ed. Francis Fawkes, 12 vols. (London, 1763), IV, 34-46.

('Twas the same Oberon, that once we saw
Circle the green, and give his dancers law.)

"Unhappy Nymph! thy beauty is thy crime—
And must such beauty perish in its prime?
No more great Henry shall enjoy those charms,
Nor thou, ill-fated Fair, adorn his arms!
Cropt like an opening rose, thy fall I fear!
But rise and supplicate the vengeance near."

Then (as methought) I wak'd with threaten'd woes,
Emerging from thick shades, a Phantom rose:
One hand sustain'd a short, but naked sword,—
And one a golden bowl, with poison stor'd:
The jealous Queen the frowning form express'd,
It spoke, and aim'd the dagger at my breast.

"Arise! nor ask thy crime—but choose thy fate,
Know prayers are vain—repentance is too late!
Vengeance is mine—Here! drink this poison'd bowl,
Or this keen dagger drinks thy guilty soul!"[51]

She awakes in horror, and, in casting about for a plan of escape, she decides to retire to a convent, only to abandon the idea because in withdrawing from the world she would lose her lover. "Love, only love, is my unbounded fault," but Heaven, she concludes, will show pity because "half of Heaven ('t is said) consists in love." In his much briefer reply Henry shows sympathy, goes over the scenes of their love, and concludes that empires and glories mean nothing compared to Rosamond's love.

Similar in form is the anonymous *Fair Rosamond to the Fair Hibernian; an Epistle* (1752), which, according to a contemporary reviewer, "contains only some general hints to the fair *Hibernian,* to caution her against the fatal effects which the ladies so often experience, from the excessive flattery and adulation of the men; to look upon *Virtue* as the chief glory of a woman; and that to tread in her paths, is the only sure road to happiness: the whole deduced from the melancholy example of the famous Rosamond."[52] Another poem in the same, but apparently more serious, vein is John Brand's *On Illicit Love. Written among the Ruins of Godstow Nunnery near Oxford* (1775). Some three of his twenty pages are given to "Contemplation" of the horror of Rosamond's sin.[53] Since the primary object of the author was,

[51] For an earlier use of the dream as a warning of danger, see below, pp. 71-2.
[52] *The Monthly Review,* VI (1752), 79. I have not seen a copy of the work.
[53] *Newcastle-upon-Tyne* (1775), pp. 5-8.

as he proclaims in his Advertisement, to "warn against the alarming Progress of Lewdness, and consequently of Licentiousness of Manners, which indeed threatens the Dissolution of our State," he has very little interest in a skillful development of the story.[54]

Although the Rosamond theme was frequently used on the stage during the time, it is remarkable that I have found no non-dramatic poem on the subject between 1775, when Brand's poem appeared, and 1854, when William Bell Scott published his "Woodstock Maze," a reflective-narrative poem of twelve ten-line stanzas in irregular tumbling verse with couplet refrain.[55] As the poem opens, Henry is conducting Fair Rosamond to the bower he has prepared for her and is explaining that she must be set apart from the world so that, like the bird and the rose, she may sing and radiate beauty. To this she protests that she much prefers simple freedom and the common pleasures of life. Nevertheless, she accepts her new way of living; but as time goes on, she becomes weary of her seclusion, and the poet, in the manner of Drayton, describes her boredom and discontent as she passes from one activity to another. She becomes nervous and apprehensive, always noting the slightest sounds about her. One evening, as she is uneasily awaiting the arrival of the king, she exclaims:

> "Hark! he comes! yet his footstep sounds
>   As it sounded never before!
> Perhaps he thinks to steal on me,
>   But I'll hide behind the door."
> She ran, she stopped, stood still as stone—
>   It was Queen Eleänore;
> And at once she felt that it was death
>   The hungering she-wolf bore!
> Oh, the leaves, brown, yellow, and red, still fall,
> Fall and fall over churchyard or hall.

In 1868 B. Montgomerie Ranking published a somewhat ambitious narrative poem, *Fair Rosamond,* which apparently met with some success with the reading public.[56] It has over 1200 lines of tumbling verse such as Coleridge employed in his *Christabel,* a work which may have provided Ranking with some of his inspiration. The attempt to inject into the poem something of the old folk flavor is not unsuccessful, and some passages have a pleasing lyrical quality. A slender plot carries

[54] For other instances of moral reflections inspired by the story, see below, pp. 44-5.

[55] *Poems, Ballads, Studies from Nature, Sonnets, etc.* (London, 1875), pp. 23-8. The poem first appeared in the author's earlier volume, *Poems by a Painter* (1854).

[56] *Fair Rosamond: and Other Poems,* 2nd ed. (London, 1869). The first edition appeared in 1868 and a third in 1876.

fairly extensive descriptive passages dealing with nature and with Rosamond's peerless beauty. The story consists of three parts, "Love's Betraying," "Rosamond's Bower," and "The King's Tryst." It begins with the meetings of Rosamond and her first lover, Hugh of Endisley, "Hereford County's pride," on the banks of the Wye. Later King Henry comes to hunt the stag in the vicinity of Clifford Town, and one day, as Hugh follows his hawk, he comes upon Henry and Rosamond as they are engaged in love-making. He cries out:

> My promised wife—can this be she!
> What hath the King to do with thee? (p. 15)

Seizing his hunting knife, he threatens the king, but Rosamond catches his arm and tells him that it is all over between them because she now loves Henry. Hugh promises to spare the king only because she loves him. In part two, Rosamond is shown in Woodstock Bower, which is described at some length. In the evening, as she sits at her spinning, she reflects upon her carefree childhood in her castle home, and she calls to mind a dream she once had had whose memory has vexed her—a dream of how a wild rose, wooed and won by a "bird in kingly mould," was sickened by the poisonous slime of a coiling snake until it drooped and died. Hardly does she finish toying with the dream of ill-omen before Queen Eleanor, following the "traitorous silken clue," appears before her and demands that she choose death by poison or dagger. Rosamond laughs jeeringly at her, declaring that Henry will soon be there. But the queen, assuring her that Henry will not come to-night, and turning a deaf ear to Rosamond's pleas for mercy, renews her command. Rosamond drinks and drops dead, and the queen quietly retires. Part three opens with Henry riding through the wood on his way to surprise his sleeping Rose. He rushes into the bower only to find her dead.

The more marked features of Ranking's story are either unusual or entirely new in the tradition. Hugh of Endisley as a lover of Rosamond is an invention of the poet suggested by the role of the rival lover first used by Warner and later developed through a number of variations. Hugh's jealousy and his act of violence against Henry, however, lead one to infer that the poet has actually assigned him the role of Queen Eleanor by simple substitution. As for Rosamond herself, she is unique in her fickleness, because no other author attempts to portray her as anything but sincere and constant in her love. The idea that Henry first met her while hunting on or near the Clifford estate is rather common after Mary Russell Mitford first referred to it in her tragedy of *Fair Rosamond*. The dream in which Rosamond is warned of her fate—

ironically recalled here too late—had been employed a number of times before.[57]

An anonymous poem, "The Death of Fair Rosamond,"[58] consisting of 132 lines of heroic couplet in the wooden and uninspired style of the minor poetry of the preceding century, appeared in the following year. It deserves only the briefest attention. Dark Eleanor's unrelenting fury and cruelty are described as she approaches defenseless Rosamond in the wood. In dumb despair Rosamond drinks poison and, after Eleanor withdraws, dies alone.

From 1869 to 1931 I know of no narrative poem dealing with the subject of Fair Rosamond. In the latter year Mr. John Masefield published his *Rose of the World,*[59] a tale that is told with originality, freshness, and economy. It exhibits the directness and vividness of a popular ballad and the sharply-etched detail and steady march of the tale-teller's art. The poet has confined the action to the queen's discovery of Henry's place of assignation and her murder of Rosamond, omitting references to the past and to political or ecclesiastical entanglements. It is a simple story of Henry, the unfaithful husband, Eleanor, the jealous wife, and Rosamond, the victim of her vengeance.

On a wild, windy night, in spite of suspicious questioning by Eleanor, Henry says he must attend a midnight council, but, as he reaches for his sword-belt,

> She pinned a tassel in his mantle's edge,
>
> A clue of white silk that would glimmer pale
> About his ankles as he trod the gale.

By means of this "token" Eleanor marks his path as he goes through the forest to Rosamond's cottage, for as she follows him she untwines "a silken floss to lead her out again." She sees Henry admitted to the cottage, and she watches and follows him home as he leaves at dawn. The next day informing him that she is going on her daily round of charity, she retraces her clue to Rosamond's cottage in the forest, gives Henry's signal knock, and, on being admitted, orders her rival either to drink the draught of poison she had prepared,

> Or I will call the hangmen who attend
>
> And they shall strip you naked and so hoot
> And beat you to the Woodstock gallows-foot
>
> Where they shall hang you.

[57] See, for example, above, p. 33 and note 51.

[58] *The Death of Fair Rosamond, and Other Poems* (London, 1869).

[59] In *Minnie Maylow's Story and Other Tales and Scenes* (New York, 1931), pp. 65-71.

Rosamond drinks the poison and dies. Eleanor lays her body on a bed and departs. That night she dreams of being choked by roses, and ever afterward she is haunted by the "scent of roses crushed." The White Nuns bury Rosamond, and for many years they show

> A little chest or scatolin of hers,
>
> Painted with birds, that Henry once had given.
> There the White Sisters prayed her into Heaven
>
> That is the rest for lovers: there they wrought
> A white-rose tomb for her from loving thought
>
> So that none thought of her, nor ever will
> Save as a lovely thing that suffered ill.

For the groundwork of his story Masefield has gone back to the original versions of the legend. For the Daedalian labyrinth, however, he has substituted the intricacies of the forest; for the traditional dagger as alternative of the poisoned bowl, the threat of whipping and hanging; and for the traditional punishment of the queen by imprisonment, the recurring dream of being choked by roses. He preserves the chronicle account of Henry's gift of the "little chest," without, however, the mystery of the moving figures; and he makes full use of the suggestion in the chronicles of the veneration of Rosamond's tomb by the nuns of Godstow who had buried her. The clue of thread, common to many versions, is nowhere else treated with so much attention as here.[60] Except for the conclusion, the entire story, as Masefield tells it, reminds one, more than certain other versions do, of a continental folk tale in which a wife who becomes suspicious of her husband's visits away from home, follows him through the forest by a clue of thread attached to his cloak, and finds him with his sweetheart.[61]

The narrative poem, the form in which the story of Fair Rosamond was established in literary tradition, after displaying symptoms of desuetude in ineffectual local poetry and Draytonian imitation, obviously suffered a sharp decline in popularity after the middle of the eighteenth century. But this decline did not occur before there had been created a fairly promising body of materials which future writers were to draw upon freely. It is pertinent, therefore, to take stock of this small literary heritage. Of the several earlier features of the story which were used in the first literary versions, the epitaph, for which the old

[60] But cf. below, pp. 60, 61, 64, 65, 90, 101 (note), 102, and especially 105.

[61] For further discussion of this tale and of its possible relation to the Rosamond story, see above, pp. 12-13.

chroniclers appear to have had a certain fondness, gradually faded out, and Rosamond's wonderful coffer, altered by Daniel and Drayton from an innocent gift to a device of seduction, and transformed by Thomas May into an entire picture gallery for the same purpose, is completely ignored by later writers before Masefield. On the other hand, the labyrinth with its bower, the clue of thread, Eleanor's jealousy and violence, Rosamond's death by poisoning, and her burial at Godstow were to become permanent features of the story. But more significant are the new growths sent out by the theme in various directions. The early literary versions furnished a number of new characters and devices, almost all of them introduced before the middle of the seventeenth century, which were to challenge the ingenuity of later writers of prose fiction and drama who were striving for originality, and which were to exert an influence in shaping the story down to the present day. The invention of new characters to complicate the action is most marked. The keeper of the bower, first created by Warner as the "Knight of trust" and rival lover, offered attractive possibilities to later writers for the development of either or both of these roles. Daniel's procuress became a favorite among writers of the chapbook. The villainous character who serves as the queen's agent to carry out her plans against Rosamond, and who first appears as Skinke in *Look about You,* assumed great importance in later versions of the story. Important suggestions for further development are to be found also in the circumstances of the first meeting of the lovers, the king's wooing in disguise, the means by which the queen gains admittance to the bower, the place of seduction prior to Rosamond's transfer to the labyrinth, Eleanor's violence and cruelty, the dream of warning which occurs to Henry or Rosamond, and the final disposition of Rosamond dead or alive. In any attempt to thread the labyrinth of literary tradition, the importance of the ballad-version can hardly be exaggerated, for its dependence upon the invention of new devices of plot made it a fertile source of suggestions for later writers. Finally, it should be pointed out that, by weaving the story into a rather ambitious historical poem, though he does not bring it into direct causal relationship with the other historical events of Henry's reign, Thomas May foreshadows its entanglement with ecclesiastical and political characters and situations which was later employed by both the dramatists and the writers of the historical novel.

CHAPTER III

PROSE FICTION

I

THE FAILURE of the narrative poem to make more than a few significant contributions to the literary tradition after the appearance of Thomas May's *Reigne of Henry the Second* (1633) was compensated by variations of the theme which were developed in the seventeenth-century chapbook. From about 1640, when the first chapbook appeared, until 1693, when the story was accorded its first dramatic treatment by Bancroft, this brief prose form no doubt did much to stimulate a continued interest in the story of Fair Rosamond and at the same time to demonstrate its potentialities for the elaboration it later underwent in the drama and novel. Through the chapbook, with its wide appeal to the reading public, the old legend was in a sense restored to the people who had been largely responsible for its creation many generations before; for the version that made its appearance in the cheap little booklets of usually twenty-four or thirty-two pages was based on the fuller accounts set down by the later chroniclers, and perhaps, too, on something that may have still lingered in oral tradition. It was, however, no longer the vague, unmotivated tale of oral tradition, but rather a somewhat ingenious version written by the anonymous hackwriter who was not unacquainted with the inventions of the early literary tradition, and who set such a value upon plot and human interest that the resulting story was fairly full-bodied, and marked by some ingenuity and originality in its minor features. Some of these minor features, by reason of the wide dissemination of the chapbook version, were eventually to be incorporated into many works of a higher order in the eighteenth and nineteenth centuries.

The story of Rosamond was certainly one of the first of the many to appear in chapbook form. "Perhaps the earliest book about this frail beauty," according to John Ashton, "is 'The Life and Death of Fair Rosamond, King Henry the Seconds Concubine, and how she was Poysoned to death by Queen Elenor. Printed for F. Coles' (circa 1640)."[1] This version continued to be issued from time to time until the middle of the nineteenth century, with varying titles, from presses all over England and Scotland—at London, Newcastle-upon-Tyne, Banbury,

[1] *Chap-books of the Eighteenth Century* (London, 1882), p. 388.

Warrington, Whitehaven, Folkirk, Kilmarnock, etc.—and ordinarily without date. A copy now before me bears witness on its title-page to the ephemeral nature of the work. Its imprint reads, curiously enough, "Newcastle upon Tyne. Printed in this present year." In spite of the varying circumstances attending the printing of so many editions through a period of two centuries, deviations among the texts are not so significant as might be expected. An examination of some fifteen different editions of the oldest and most popular version reveals that although the general plan of the story is essentially the same throughout, there are changes of phrasing, interpolated moral pronouncements, and remarks upon the historicity of certain features of the story. There is clearly little attempt to disguise the fact that editions plagiarize one another. Historical events in general, and political situations in particular, in the reign of Henry the Second, which were used concurrently in the drama and novel to complicate plot and give reality to the story, are either definitely subordinated or completely avoided.

For this study I have had access to no edition that can with certainty be said to antedate the eighteenth century. Of the two independent versions discussed here, the earlier, which first appeared in print about 1640, may be outlined as follows:[2] Fair Rosamond, the daughter of Lord Walter Clifford, was so beautiful that "she was not only the public and common discourse of our own nation, but even the table talk of remote countries and foreign people." After praising the beauty of a woman he had seen, King Henry is so inflamed with curiosity by Rosamond's uncle's description of her than he compels the uncle reluctantly to reveal her name and her place of residence. Soon thereafter his Majesty makes a progress into Oxfordshire and invites himself to the Clifford home, where he falls in love with Rosamond. After three days with her he is compelled to leave for France. Upon receiving a letter from the king and being uncertain of her course, Rosamond consults her governess, Alethea, who encourages her to "send him a comfortable answer." Lady Clifford discovers the royal letter and reveals it to her husband. They both immediately upbraid Rosamond for her boldness, but, being assured that she is still innocent, she is made to promise to entertain a suit from Lord Fitzwalters. News of King Henry's return from Normandy, however, prompts her to discourage

[2] I follow the text of *The History of the Life and Death of Fair Rosamond, King Henry II. Concubine. Shewing, How Queen Eleanor plotted to destroy Fair Rosamond, to prevent which, she was removed to a stately bower at Woodstock, near Oxford; and while the King was in France, fair Rosamond was poisoned by Queen Eleanor. Newcastle upon Tyne. Printed in this present year.* This is apparently an early nineteenth-century edition (cf. BM 1079, i. 24. [23]) of the earliest version, *The Life and Death of Fair Rosamond,* of about 1640. It consists of 24 pages (including the title-page) and is divided into seven chapters, to each of which is prefixed an argument.

Lord Fitzwalters's attentions. Her parents, alarmed at this turn of events, send her with Alethea, "the false governess," to the home of a kinsman in Cornwall. Informed of Rosamond's whereabouts by Alethea, the king commands Rosamond's uncle to fetch her to court, where she is placed in private lodgings with Alethea. Although he is aided by Alethea's wiles and persuasions, the king grows impatient of his repeated failure to win Rosamond's complete surrender to him. Finally, Alethea contrives to have him take her place at night in Rosamond's bed, and he seduces her. After many such "wanton dalliances in private," Queen Eleanor, unable to wean the king from his new mistress, makes such threats that he appoints a "guard to wait on [Rosamond] at home and abroad," and later builds for her at great cost a "stately palace, called the delightful Bower of Woodstock." This so enrages the queen that she incites Prince Richard to raise a rebellion against his father in France. Before leaving to put down the rebellion, the king places Sir Thomas, Rosamond's uncle, in charge of the bower. As soon as the king goes abroad, the queen with her trusted confederates rides posthaste to Woodstock, has Sir Thomas and his party killed, and seizes the clue of thread which directs her to Rosamond, who confesses her fault and asks for compassion on her unborn child. The queen in a rage offers her "the choice either to drink the cup of poison she has prepared for her, or die by the sword." Rosamond drinks the poison and dies. Upon his return the king, stricken with grief, orders all the queen's aids to be "apprehended, convicted, and put to the most cruel tortures," and he spares the queen's life only because she is a foreign princess. She is, however, "confined for life-time in a strict imprisonment" and the king commands that if she should die in prison "her body should not be buried, but there moulder to dust." He caused Rosamond's body to be removed from "that obscure cave, in which the queen had caused her to be laid, and buried with all the funeral pomp imaginable, at Godstow, near Oxford, [and he] erected to her memory a stately Tomb, on which was this inscription.

> Within this Tomb lies the world's chiefest rose;
> She who was sweet, will now offend your nose."

Though there is little reason to assume that the edition I am using differs in any essential from the earliest version printed about 1640, of which I have not seen a copy, some of my inferences regarding the relationship of this version to the tradition must be regarded as tentative. The problem is further complicated by our inability to determine the date of the ballad, *The Unfortunate Concubine; or, Rosamond's Overthrow* (first printed in 1723), with which the present version has certain features in common. For example, the opening episode of each version, in which the king is so inflamed by praise of Rosamond's beauty as to go in search of her at her home, carries the memory back ultimately to Greene's "Shepherd's Tale" in *The Mourning Garment* (1590).[3] But the chapbook here bears a closer relationship to the ballad, in which the praiser is also a relative—Rosamond's brother—who is sent by the king to fetch the beauty to court.[4] On the other hand, certain features of the present version clearly antedate even the earliest edition of the chapbook. Alethea, "the false governess," though her name is an addition, is a considerably more elaborated character than Daniel's "seeming matron" and Drayton's "wicked woman," and bears a fairly close relationship to Thomas May's "Ancient Dame" in her wily role as procuress.[5] The exchange of letters between the king and Rosamond may have been suggested, though not necessarily, by Drayton's poems in *England's Heroical Epistles* (1597). The "private lodgings," in which Rosamond was housed and eventually seduced by Henry with the aid of Alethea, had earlier appeared as "a sollitarie Grange" in Daniel and as "a faire retreat" in May. The labyrinth to which she was later removed is so much more minutely described here than in any earlier version, perhaps because readers of chapbooks would be curious about such a wonder, that I give the account in full:

> [King Henry] caused a stately palace, called the delightful Bower of Woodstock, in Oxfordshire, to be built with great cost; with all the cunning turnings and Windings imaginable, far exceeding the delalion [*sic*] Labrinth, which he appointed for her country retirement when she pleased to take the air. The stately Bower had many entries and passages under ground, into which light came thro' narrow stone crevices, shaded with bushes not perceivable to those that walked above, rising with doors in hills far distant, to escape from danger, upon any timely notice, tho' the place should be suddenly beseiged and surrounded: and within this stately Bower were intricate mazes and windings thro' long entries, rooms, and gallerys, strongly secured with 152 doors; so that to find the way into the remote apartments, the skilful artist had left a silver clew of thread, without the Guidance of which, it was impossible to be done. About this bower were curious gardens, fountains, and a wilderness, and all manner of delights for pleasant situation and recreation, to furnish it out as another earthly paradise, for so fair a creature to inhabit: and thither the king often resorted to see his beloved Rosamond.[6]

Certainly one detail—the reference to "152 doors"—suggests that the writer had read the description in Deloney's *Mournful Dittie*, "Whenas

[3] See above, p. 15, note 6.
[4] For a discussion of the ballad, see above, pp. 30-2.
[5] See above, pp. 17, 21, 25-6.
[6] *The History of the Life and Death*, p. 19.

King Henry rul'd this land,"[7] but the author of the chapbook gives his reader a much more minute description of this curious wonder than any of his predecessors had done. That he is actually dependent upon Deloney's ballad for other ideas is clear from the facts that the keeper is called Sir Thomas—that he is Rosamond's uncle, however, who initiated the whole action of the story, is a new feature—and that he is set upon by Eleanor's confederates, though in Deloney's ballad he is not actually slain. Rosamond's burial at Godstow, the monument erected to her memory, and the imprisonment of the queen follow common tradition. Naturally enough, the writer of the chapbook, having the popular reader in mind, substitutes for the Latin version of Rosamond's epitaph what appears to be an original English paraphrase.

Several of the episodes of the story appear to be new in the tradition: the visit of the king to the Clifford manor, the dispatch of Rosamond and Alethea to the home of a kinsman in Cornwall, and the seduction-scene, in which Alethea substitutes the king for herself in Rosamond's bed. The suit of Lord Fitz Walters (in other editions variously given as Fitzwalter, Fitzwaters, and Fitzwarren) could hardly have been derived from Warner's "Knight of trust" who was for a brief moment a would-be rival lover. It is more likely that his role as a rival lover, which is given considerable prominence in the chapbook version, was an invention of the writer to complicate the plot. In this version, too, the queen for the first time offers Rosamond a choice of a cup of poison or death by the sword—an option which became a permanent feature of every later version in which Rosamond met her death at the queen's hands. Rosamond's reference to her unborn child in her plea to Eleanor is the first hint we have in any literary version that she was ever with child by Henry.[8] Finally, a curious allusion to an "obscure cave, in which the queen had caused [Rosamond] to be laid," taken together with Henry's emotional reaction upon hearing of Rosamond's murder, would suggest that the writer may have known the *French Chronicle of London*,[9] or that these ingredients of the story still lingered on in oral tradition.

Four other editions of *The Life and Death* need now to be examined to ascertain significant variations which occur among them. To facilitate reference, I shall use alphabetical symbols as follows:

[7] See above, p. 22.

[8] Sir John Ferne, in his *Blazon of Gentrie* (London, 1586), p. 89, is the first, I believe, to designate William Longsword and Geoffrey, Archbishop of York, as natural sons of Henry and Rosamond. The claim to priority of the two items mentioned above rests, of course, upon the assumption that the edition from which I am quoting corresponds in pertinent passages with seventeenth-century editions of the text.

[9] See above, pp. 9ff.

A. *The History of the Life and Death of Fair Rosamond* . . . Newcastle upon Tyne, *n. d.* Pp. 24. Full title of this chapbook is given above, p. 40, note 2.
B. "The Loves of King Henry II, and Fair Rosamond," in *A Select Collection of Novels and Histories in Six Volumes.* By several eminent hands. [Ed. Samuel Croxall.] London, 1729, IV, 203-35.
C. *The Unfortunate Concubines; the History of Fair Rosamond, Mistress to Henry II. and Jane Shore, Concubine to Edward IV. Kings of England. Shewing How They Came to Be so. With Their lives, Remarkable Actions, and Unhappy Ends. Extracted from Eminent Records, and the Whole Illustrated with Cuts Suitable to Each Subject.* London: Printed for R. Ware at the Bible and Sun, Ludgate Hill; C. Hitch, at the Red-Lion in Pater-noster-Row; and J. Hodges at the Looking Glass, London-Bridge. 1748. Pp. 165. The Rosamond story occupies pp. 1-78. B. M. lists a 1717 ed. (12330.a.24.).
D. *Fair Rosamond; or, The Bower of Woodstock.* London: Orlando Hodgson, 111, Fleet Street [1824?]. Pp. 23 + 1 blk.
E. *The History of Fair Rosamond, otherwise Eleanor* [sic] *Clifford, and Her Royal Paramour, Henry the Second, with an Affecting Account of Her Melancholy and Horrible Death, at the Hands of the Injured Queen Eleanor, in the Bower at Woodstock.* Durham: Printed by G. Walker, Jun., Sadler Street, 1838. Rosamond story occupies pages 1-18.

The author of *The Loves of King Henry II* (B) devotes the first six pages of his version to a denunciation of the outrages committed by tyrants against their subjects. Later he discusses the question whether Rosamond was the real name of Henry's mistress, or whether, as Holinshed seems to imply, the name was given her by the common people (B., p. 214); and he has grave doubts as to the actual existence of the labyrinth, adding, "Yet are we not to Wonder, that the Monkish Historians should deliver down to us a Tale of such Absurdity; when the same Chroniclers tell Us that, in the King's Reign, a Dragon of Marvellous Bigness was seen at St. *Osyths'* in *Essex,* which, by its very Motion, set many Houses and Buildings on Fire" (p. 227). Moreover, after completing his tragic story, he concludes that such is the end, according to some accounts. But "others pretend to tell us, that when the Queen once saw her, she only reprov'd her for her criminal Familiarity with the King, and did her no other Damage; but that *Rosamond* retir'd into a Nunnery at Godstow near Woodstock, where after a short Continuance she dy'd a natural Death, and there was buried" (p. 232; cf. C., pp. 72-3). The author of *The Unfortunate Concubines* (C), on the other hand, sees in the story a forceful warning to maidens against whoredom under any circumstances whatsoever:

> Perhaps the Splendor of her Living and the Part they still bear in the World, may make others, as well as themselves, think they are guilty of

no Crime; but them that shall read the following History, will find that every Miss, how rich or poor soever she be, yet if she lives in Adultery and Whoredom, is as much, if not more guilty, than *Rosamond* and *Jane Shore:* For of either of these it may be said, they sought not the Royal Favour; but endeavoured to avoid it, is [*sic*] much as possible; and were both of them betrayed by those whom they trusted: King *Henry* being brought into *Rosamond's* bed by her Governess *Alethea,* both without her Knowledge, and then while she was a sleep . . . Not that I hereby go about to excuse [her] . . . Fair *Rosamond* was willing to taste the Pleasure of the Court, and yet perhaps believed she could have kept herself from the Pollutions of it. But she beforehand knew the King had a great Kindness for her; and had the fatall Consequence of it too plainly laid before her by her Parents, to make the least Defence for what she did by pleading Ignorance . . . Let me therefore commend this History to the curious Perusal of all that would avoid Occasions of Sin . . . They that imagine *Rosamond* happy in her Bower, let them behold her trembling with a Cup of Poison in her Hands, and in vain begging to be deliver'd from the dreadful Draught: And when she had drank it, let them behold the Triumphs of Death over Beauty: And see what Disorders it makes in Nature, how her late beautiful Face is disfigur'd, and the Rose on her Cheeks all dead and withering, her Eyes distorted, and her whole Body swelled up, and labouring under horrid Convulsions: And who would change Conditions with her now? And yet all this is but the Shell and Out-Side, the least part of the Wages of Sin.[10]

Certain minor variations are also to be noted. Some editions open with a brief account of the reigns of Henry I, Stephen, and Henry II.[11] Other interpolations are accounts of the costly gifts sent to Rosamond, and of the bribing of Alethea at the Clifford home;[12] of Eleanor's dropping of threatening letters at court,[13] and of having a postboy deliver a letter, presumably from the king, to Sir Thomas, the keeper, in order to create an opportunity to slay him at the signal of a horn-blast.[14] These variations are new in the tradition. Two others, however, are derivative: Rosamond's plea to be allowed to accompany Henry to France disguised as his page,[15] which is apparently an invention of Deloney and which appears in more elaborate form in Bancroft's *Henry the Second* (1693);[16] and Rosamond's warning of her fate in her dream of the infuriated queen[17] which is to be found in Bancroft also.

[10] Preface. Cf. *History of Jane Shore, Concubine to Edward IV* . . . Printed and sold by W. and T. Fordyce, 15, Grey Street (Newcastle, *n. d.*), pp. 23-4.

[11] See C., ch. i; D., pp. 3-4; E., pp. 2-3.

[12] B., pp. 215-16; C., ch. iii; D., p. 6; E., p. 4.

[13] C., ch. v; D., pp. 17-18; E., p. 13.

[14] C., ch. vii; D., p. 21; E., p. 16.

[15] C., ch. vi; D., p. 20.

[16] See above, p. 22, and below, p. 71.

[17] C., ch. vii, D., p. 21; E., pp. 15-16.

These differences indicate that an author who set about the revision of an old chapbook for printing felt free to improve his new edition by interposing his political views, or by indulging his eighteenth-century skepticism of "monkish history," or by directing attention to the moral to be drawn from Fair Rosamond's tragedy. They show also that he did not hesitate to incorporate into the story any newly-invented device he may have recalled from his reading of versions of a higher literary order. No doubt some of the minor items of this kind were most widely disseminated among nineteenth-century authors who came upon them in the popular chapbooks.

The History of Fair Rosamond, the Beautiful Mistress of King Henry the Second,[18] a nineteenth-century creation, does not end in tragedy, and it differs in so many essentials from *The Life and Death* version just discussed that it may be regarded as an almost independent work. In an obvious attempt to appear historical, it begins like a biography: Rosamond, daughter of Walter Lord Clifford, was born in 1134, and was at the age of ten or eleven received into Godstow Nunnery as a boarder. There, or rather at Medley Fair nearby, Henry met her when he was fifteen and she but twelve years of age.[19] Later he would often stray from his tutor at Oxford, and Rosamond from the precincts of Godstow, to pass an hour together. At sixteen Henry had to assert his claim to the throne, but after he had laid aside his armor, not wishing to encounter Lord Clifford, who favored the suit of Lord Fitzwarren, he met her as he was hunting in the vicinity of her father's castle. He urged flight, but she refused. For her obstinacy in refusing Lord Fitzwarren's suit, her father sent her again to Godstow Nunnery, and besought her to take the veil. Later her confessor, Father Ambrose, who had previously informed Henry of her love, placed in her hand a note from her lover advising her to follow the advice of her confessor. [Explanation of the bigotry of the age, pp. 12-13.] Rosamond escaped from the Nunnery with Henry, but upon their arrival at Uxbridge she begged to be returned to her parents. Instead, Henry took her to London and lodged her in an apartment amid the cloisters of the Knights Templars. Again she pleaded to go home, but Henry quieted and seduced her. At length she gave birth to a son, and Henry, called away by the death of King Stephen, and seeming to forget his promise to wed her, married Eleanor of Aquitane. He sent Rosamond a note telling her

[18] The title continues: "Derived from the Most Authentic Sources. Her Birth, and Education at the Nunnery at Godstow, and First Meeting with Prince Henry; Her Escape from the Nunnery: Her Seduction, and Subsequent Residence at Woodstock: Her Interview with Queen Eleanor, and her Death. Derby: Thomas Richardson." (B. M. 12612. aaa. 3., dated [1846?].)

[19] P. 4. But cf. p. 3, where the date is given as 1149.

that he still loved her alone. She soon became for a second time a mother. Though she had resolved never to see Henry again, he forced himself into her presence, and they were reconciled. The ensuing jealousy of the queen compelled Henry to remove Rosamond to Woodstock Palace, where he had Theodore D'Agneville, a Norman architect, render her abode impervious to her enemies. Later, while Henry was in France putting down Richard's rebellion, D'Agneville sought to make love to Rosamond, but was spurned. In revenge, he admitted Queen Eleanor to Rosamond's apartment. The beauty and meekness of Rosamond so won the heart of the queen that the weapon dropped from her hand. Rosamond promised to see Henry no more, and to enter Godstow Nunnery. The queen then left, and the next day Rosamond entered the Nunnery, where she lived a blameless life. When Henry returned, he was frenzied to learn that Rosamond was now beyond his reach forever. He never forgave the queen, and spent his remaining days in warring against her and her sons. He died July 6, 1189, and Rosamond expired in the year 1191, and was buried with great solemnity at Godstow.

The only feature of this version clearly linking it with the older one is the episode dealing with the suit of Lord Fitzwarren. It should not be overlooked, however, that Lord Clifford's secluding Rosamond from Henry by sending her a second time to Godstow may have some connection with her enforced visit to Cornwall for the same purpose in the older version. It is much more probable, however, that this idea was derived from Thomas Miller's *Fair Rosamond* (1839), in which Rosamond is a boarder at Godstow, is rescued from drowning by Henry, and later marries him. Miller may also have been responsible for the introduction of Henry and Rosamond's two children, although by this date various sources could have been drawn upon for that detail.[20] On the other hand, the meeting of Henry and Rosamond at Medley Fair and their flight later to London do not appear in earlier accounts. Other elements of the story bear only vague, if any, resemblance to characters and incidents met with before. The apartment in the cloisters of the Knights Templars is perhaps some vestige of Daniel's "sollitarie Grange," May's "faire retreat of greater privacy," or the "private lodgings" of the earlier chapbook, but nothing more. To account for some of the other features of the story, we have to anticipate works discussed in the following chapters. Father Ambrose, for example, as a villainous ecclesiastic who betrays confessional secrecy, will recall the Abbot and Bertrard in Bancroft's *Henry the Second* (1693)[21] but he is not, like the Abbott, an enemy of the lovers in the service of the queen; he is

[20] See below, p. 51.
[21] See below, pp. 69ff.

rather a male Alethea furthering their affair. The young Norman architect, Theodore D'Agneville, who fills the traditional role of the rival lover, has, however, no exact counterpart as the avenger of his rejection by treachery, except possibly in the character of Leicester in Hawkins's *Henry and Rosamond* (1749).[22] Finally, Eleanor's merciful impulse to spare Rosamond does not proceed from a premeditated plan to trick or frighten her into retirement at Godstow, as in Addison and Hawkins,[23] but from the pacifying effect of Rosamond's beauty and meekness.

The author of this late chapbook is apparently motivated by the idea, which became increasingly prominent among nineteenth-century writers, that since the legend involves actual characters and incidents, it should be made as far as possible historically plausible. His use of dates, omission of the marvellous and the fabulous, introduction of the priest, and avoidance of tragedy—all these point in this direction. By the date of the appearance of this chapbook, the historical novel as written by Sir Walter Scott and others had revealed to its readers a new relationship between history and fiction, and writers of the historical romance were not slow to make use of it in their handling of the Fair Rosamond theme.

II

At the beginning of the nineteenth century conditions were conducive to the development of the Rosamond story in the form of the historical novel. The narrative poem, the ballad, the chapbook, and the work of antiquaries had all served to popularize and enrich the theme, and eighteenth-century dramatic versions of it had demonstrated that it possessed considerable possibilities for the more intricate and detailed plot-construction demanded by the historical prose romance. As an indication of both literary and historical interest in the story one may cite a collection of miscellanea published about 1790 by an anonymous compiler as *The Unfortunate Royal Mistresses, Rosamond Clifford, and Jane Shore, Concubines to King Henry the Second, and Edward the Fourth,*[24] in which were brought together a variety of items designed to satisfy the curiosity of those readers who had developed a more than ordinary interest in the tragic fate of the two

[22] See below, pp. 75-6.

[23] See below, pp. 72-7.

[24] The title continues: "with historical and metrical memoirs of those celebrated persons. By Sir Thomas More, Michael Drayton, Thomas Hearne, &c. London: Printed by and for William Cole, 10, Newgate Street." n. d. Since William Cole was in Newgate Street between 1765 and 1792, and since the latest identifiable date in the work is 1787, I should regard 1790 as the approximate date of its publication.

famed but unfortunate royal mistresses. A brief exposition of what the various chronicles report on Rosamond is followed by Deloney's ballad; a reprint of Stephens's remarks about Godstow Nunnery from Dugdale's *Monasticon;* the ballad, *The Unfortunate Concubine; or, Rosamond's Overthrow;* the "Epistles" of Rosamond and Henry by Drayton; "Memoirs of Queen Eleanor;" a ballad titled "Queen Eleanor's Confession;" and a four-page "brief history" of Fair Rosamond "from the pen of a celebrated modern writer."

All of these have been previously noticed in this study except the last, whose author I have not been able to identify. The peculiar features of it are that Henry met Rosamond accidentally "among the galaxy of fine women that adorned his court," that Queen Eleanor bribed Henry's "confidential servant to hint the cause of his alienated affections" and "to betray the abode of poor Rosamond," that she allowed Rosamond to write Henry a letter after she had drunk the poison, and that Henry "died of a broken heart, and at the hour of her dissolution, consoled himself by reflecting, that he should at least meet his mistress in heaven."[25] The author greatly simplifies the plot of the story, by omitting any mention of a procuress or place of seduction or of a rival lover, and by making the queen's task of getting at Rosamond a relatively easy one. He seems more intent upon directing the reader's attention to the beauty of the relationship between the two lovers. In her proud Palace at Woodstock,

> fair Rosamond bloomed like a rose amid a wilderness of sweets. She had the entire devotion of the proudest monarch of his day, the respect of the finest women of her time. Had you lived in that auspicious aera, you might have seen the sweet girl hanging fondly on the arm of her enamoured lover, and wandering in the glorious hour of twilight, through the darkling groves of Woodstock, where, after the busy turmoil of the court was over, the monarch would love to retire; and while in the presence of his dear Rosamond, forgot even the miseries of his domestic life. He loved to sit and hear her warble the ditties of her native land, and would often place himself beside her for hours, twining her glossy ringlets in his hand, or breathing the vows of transport in the ear of the happy one. Months tolled on, and every day seemed but to dawn on the increasing fervor of his affection. Never were such a fond couple yet seen.[26]

The letter which Rosamond was permitted to write to Henry is designed also to enhance the enduring quality of her love:

> Henry, my own dear Henry, we must part for ever; a poisonous reptile has stung your poor Rosamond to death, and she will never again behold you. But do not forget me, love; sometimes visit the grave where

[25] Pp. 60-4.
[26] Pp. 60-1.

> she who was once your's, now reposes, and her spirit will yet be happy; for if souls are ever permitted to re-visit earth, I will come to you, and talk of the happiness of our re-union. Henry, I can write to you no more, I am already dying; but the last fond name that trembles on my lips, shall be the dear, dear name of Henry.[27]

In his ignoring of all moral considerations and romanticizing the beauty of the royal affair, the author foreshadows the attitude adopted by later writers of the historical novel.

Among these, first mention is owed to Sir Walter Scott. Strangely enough, he did not devote a novel to the subject, but the theme obviously intrigued him, and he many times refers to the story and to places associated with Rosamond in his novel *Woodstock* (1826). There can be little doubt, too, that the popularity of his historical romances in general prompted other writers to view the story of Rosamond as offering attractive material for treatment in that type of fiction which had brought him fame.

The first of these novelists was Thomas Miller, who published in 1839 a three-volume historical romance titled *Fair Rosamond; or, The Days of King Henry II*,[28] a work which occupies an important place in the development of the Rosamond story because of the new and attractive role assigned to Thomas À. Becket. In his drama, *Henry the Second* (1693), John Bancroft was the first author to make use of the struggle between church and state in Henry's reign to complicate the plot of the love story. He represents disgruntled ecclesiastical partisans of the martyred Becket as the agents of Queen Eleanor in effecting her nefarious plans to murder Rosamond. In this he was followed by Thomas Hull in his play, *The Fall of Rosamond* (1774). William Henry Ireland's *Henry the Second* (1799) shows an advance over his predecessors as the first work actually to bring Becket himself into entanglement with the story of Rosamond by revealing him in conspiracy with Eleanor against the lovers. In all these dramatic versions extending over more than a century of time, Becket's partisans or Becket himself is represented not merely in opposition to the king, but in active support of the queen's schemes against Fair Rosamond. In Thomas Miller's novel, on the other hand, Becket appears as the friend and priestly protector of the queen's rival, as one who is inclined to condone the illicit love affair as one which cannot be helped, while he seeks to forestall the evil consequences which he fears may come of it.

As the novel opens, Rosamond, who is a boarder at Godstow Nunnery, is rescued by Henry, whose identity is unknown to her, from drowning in the waters of the Glyne. Soon thereafter they are secretly

[27] P. 63.

[28] London, 1839.

married, and Eleanor, whose suspicions are aroused by Henry's attentions to Rosamond, sends her retainer, one Oliphant Ugglethred, to Woodstock to spy on Henry's actions. Becket advises the king to hide Rosamond in Normandy—a plan never carried out. Ugglethred steals into Rosamond's apartment at night, but she flees to the Park, where she is overtaken by Henry's enemies and conveyed to the White Fortress now being beseiged by the royal army. Rosamond's father, but recently returned from Palestine, where he had gone after learning of his daughter's rash marriage, is killed before her eyes by a stone hurled by Henry's troops. Henry eventually takes the Fortress, recovers Rosamond, and, in return for Becket's defense of his love affair to Queen Eleanor, promises him the primacy. At Becket's suggestion Rosamond is placed, with Maud, her maid, in the labyrinth at Woodstock, where she gives birth to a child named William. Meantime, Henry has been having his troubles with Becket, now archbishop, and when Rosamond is informed of the fact, she attempts to mollify his anger against the primate by taking his part; but Henry's extreme rage causes her to desist. Henry promises her to go to Rome to secure a divorce from Queen Eleanor. One day while Pierre Vidal, the minstrel, is talking with Maud, Ugglethred carries off young William to Oxford, where Eleanor is prevented from stabbing the child by the sudden arrival of Henry, who wrenches the dagger from her hand and strikes her a blow which leaves her senseless on the floor. Ugglethred, however, escapes, but young William is returned to his mother. As a result of further quarrels of Henry and Becket, the latter is compelled to flee the country. But before he goes, he visits Rosamond at Woodstock and she again attempts in vain to serve as peacemaker between her two champions. He asks her to accompany him to France, promising that she will be treated as his child. This she refuses to do, as she thinks of her second child, Geoffrey. He gives her his blessing by placing "his hands upon her beautiful head," and then rides away. Rosamond has forebodings of harm as Henry bids her farewell on his leaving for France. He promises her to be reconciled to Becket, and leaves for Normandy. Taking advantage of his absence from the country, Queen Eleanor hies to Woodstock and after many difficulties and unsuccessful attempts to reach Rosamond, finally, through the aid of Ugglethred, discovers her sitting by the river with Maud. At the queen's approach Rosamond flees into the labyrinth, but the queen, getting the clue from a scarlet silk girdle left behind, manages to overtake her in the bower. Unable to force Rosamond to confess to her secret marriage to Henry, Eleanor compels her to choose between the dagger and a cup of poison. Rosamond drinks the draught and swoons. Eleanor is taken prisoner by Rosamond's attendants and led back to Woodstock Palace. Upon his return from abroad, Henry, after visiting Woodstock, begs to be conducted to Godstow Nunnery to visit Rosamond's grave in the chapel. Henry is as surprised as the reader to find that Rosamond is still alive and is now a nun. She shows him her face for the last time and retires into the convent. The surprising resurrection of Rosamond, we are told, is to be explained by the fact that the potion which she had drunk had been rendered harmless by Ugglethred, who in preparing it had left out the poison. Maud and Pierre Vidal are married, but the queen is imprisoned for the remainder of King Henry's reign.

In view of the late date of Miller's novel we may pass over his use of any features of the story that had been of common occurrence in the literary tradition. However, at least three omissions of important traditional devices are noteworthy. He had no need of a procuress or procurer, and even less of a seduction-episode, because these are dispensed with by the arrangement of a secret marriage at the outset. Moreover, since he apparently regards Oliphant Ugglethred's cleverness as a ferret sufficiently adequate for discovering the secret ways of the labyrinth, he provides no keeper of the bower who must practice treachery, or who has to be tricked or slain, or both. Finally, he introduces no rival lover, though Becket's regard for Fair Rosamond was sufficiently warm to suggest to a later writer a considerable development of him in that unpriestlike role.[29] On the other hand, he did derive certain important ideas from his predecessors. Oliphant Ugglethred, whose primordial ancestor was Skinke in *Look About You* (1600), is no doubt drawn from John Bancroft's Bertrard in *Henry the Second* (1693), but he differs from Bertrard in his failure to become the complete villain when he omits the poison from Eleanor's potion. From the same author, Miller derived the scene in which Eleanor's dagger-thrust at young William is prevented by the timely arrival of Henry.[30] His greatest debt, however, is to Joseph Addison's opera, *Rosamond* (1707), to which may be ultimately traced every transformation of the tragedy of Rosamond into a tragi-comedy or farce. To him Miller owes some slight debt for that pair of lovers, Maud the maid and Vidal the minstrel, who are little more than innocent spectators amid action charged with potential tragedy. However, except that they are a pair of lovers who are close to the royal pair but on a lower level, they bear little resemblance to Addison's Sir Trusty and Grideline, the comic keeper and the maid who parody their betters. More important is Miller's acceptance of Addison's plan for averting the tragedy that tradition had imposed upon Fair Rosamond. There is one important difference, however. Whereas Addison's Eleanor knowingly administers an innocuous draught in order to convey the unconscious form of her rival to safe-keeping in Godstow Nunnery, Miller's Eleanor is tricked

[29] See Mrs. Kate Charlotte Maberly, *The Lady and the Priest*, below, pp. 56ff.

[30] For a discussion of Bancroft's play, see below, pp. 69ff.

into a mock murder by the very agent who had brought her to her victim.

But the new features contributed to the tradition are more numerous, and some of them are of the greatest importance for us in understanding certain later developments of the story; for to sustain the interest of the reader of a comparatively simple story through a three-volume novel, it was necessary for the author to face and deal with the necessity of making departures from well-established practices and of introducing new inventions of plot and character. The opening episode, in which Henry rescues Rosamond from drowning in the Glyne near Godstow Nunnery, in which she is a boarder, is of Miller's invention. The same statement applies to the secret marriage and Eleanor's futile attempt to make Rosamond confess to it; to Lord Clifford's pilgrimage to the Holy Land and the manner of his death; and to Henry's last interview with Rosamond at Godstow. Henry and Rosamond's sons, William and Geoffrey, are new characters in the literary tradition, although in the old seventeenth-century chapbooks Rosamond pleads with Eleanor for her unborn child, and in Mary Russell Mitford's *Fair Rosamond* (1827) reference is made by Rosamond to her two children, though they are not introduced as characters into the play. In the light of later developments of the story this is a significant innovation, because many later writers in the nineteenth century made much of these child characters. Another invention which was to become popular later is represented in the episodes relating the abduction of Rosamond and the kidnapping of young William. Finally, the most radical departure from commonly accepted practice is to be observed in the new conception of the character of Becket. As I have already indicated, in Ireland's *Henry the Second* (1799), the only previous version of the Rosamond story in which the archbishop actually appears, he is cast in the role of abettor of Eleanor's machinations against both Henry and Rosamond. In Miller's novel, on the other hand, not only does Becket wink at Henry's bigamy by twice suggesting measures for Rosamond's protection and by defending the king's actions in order to allay the queen's suspicions, but he becomes a fatherly protector of Rosamond and begs her to flee to France with him. She, in turn, assumes the role of friend to Becket as well as lover of Henry, and consequently seeks on several occasions to reconcile the two great adversaries. Years later, this new relationship between Rosamond and Becket becomes one of the most attractive features of Tennyson's most successful play.

Five years after the appearance of Miller's work, Pierce Egan the younger published his *Fair Rosamond*.[31] He is clearly heavily indebted to Miller for many of his ideas, but he has so entangled the Rosamond

[31] London, 1844.

theme with the violence and outlawry of the feudal period that his novel gives all the appearance of an independent work. The story revolves about Rosamond, who dominates the entire action of the novel, although incidents of plotting, intrigue, and violence swell each episode of the work. In contrast to Miller's novel, Egan's does not introduce Becket, who is alluded to but twice. As the novel opens, Henry, Duke of Anjou, travelling *incognito* in the vicinity of Clifford Castle, rescues Rosamond's maid, Algitha, from a retainer of Baron Reymond Le Gros, who as a rejected suitor has plotted to abduct Rosamond. As a result of this action Henry meets Fair Rosamond and secretly reveals to her his true identity, and they fall in love. Later, coming upon her by chance in the woods, he is surprised in his interview by the approach of Lord Clifford and Prince Eustace, son of King Stephen, a suitor who is favored by Clifford but loathed by Rosamond. The prince picks a quarrel with Henry, who humiliates him by twice disarming him. In revenge, Prince Eustace uses forged letters to convince Lord Clifford that Rosamond has had illicit relations with "the young knave" Henry, and Clifford, taken in by the trick, vows that she shall marry Prince Eustace forthwith. Upon his learning of the plot, Henry meets Rosamond at night and is married to her by an old priest. She is removed for safety to the castle of Ethered Ironsides. Later, accompanied by his faithful friend, Hubert de St. Clair, Henry returns to Normandy, where Le Gros gives him convincing proof that Rosamond has had an affair with Prince Eustace. Hubert, who is dispatched to England to investigate the matter, is promptly thrown into prison as an enemy of King Stephen, and Henry, now believing the worst, has his marriage annulled, and weds Eleanor of Aquitaine. Soon thereafter, upon King Stephen's death, Henry becomes king of England, and after the coronation Hubert, now released from prison, visits Rosamond and becomes convinced of her absolute innocence of the charges Le Gros had made. Henry becomes reconciled to her and decides to place her where he can visit her frequently. Meantime Eleanor, who has become suspicious of Henry's concern for Rosamond, engages Le Gros as her agent to help her rid herself of her rival. He sends a ruffian to Ethered's castle to abduct Rosamond, but the ruffian is captured by Aldred and turned over to Hubert. Hubert then brings Rosamond and her maid Algitha to Woodstock, where Henry declares her to be his true and lawful wife and promises to divorce Eleanor if Rosamond wishes to become the acknowledged queen of England. This she steadfastly refuses, preferring to live in retirement. The queen and Le Gros are tricked into the belief that Rosamond is residing at Arundel Castle, and when Le Gros tries to reach her there, he is wounded by Hubert but escapes to London. Meanwhile, Aldred conducts Lord Clifford to Rosamond. He is unsuccessful in his attempt to persuade her to advance her claim to share the throne with Henry. Eleanor next turns her attention to the labyrinth, in which her intended victim is concealed. After many unsuccessful attempts to learn its secrets she and Le Gros and her Saracen slave, Saladan, surprise Rosamond sitting alone with her child. By threatening to kill the child, Eleanor seeks to extract from Rosamond a written denial that she ever married Henry, but, failing this, she and her slave prepare to murder her. At that very moment Aldred, Rosamond's faithful guard, who has just dispatched Le Gros as he hid in the bushes outside, arrives to kill the slave and take Eleanor prisoner. At Rosamond's command the queen is reluctantly released by Aldred, and the king arrives upon the scene. After Rosamond recovers from her fright, she makes Henry promise to return to Eleanor, and she retires to Godstow Nunnery, where the king was permitted only once more to see her face—the day before she took the veil. Aldred came into Le Gros' estate, Lord Clifford never again left his castle, and Hubert died at the siege of Bridgenorth in Shropshire when he stepped into the path of an arrow intended for his king.

It will be noted that the similarities here to Miller's work, especially in those ideas which he introduced into the story for the first time, are numerous and significant for the study of the creative processes of prolific writers. In Miller's novel, Henry, *incognito,* rescues Rosamond from drowning, whereas in Egan, as Henry travels *incognito* through the country, he rescues her maid, Algitha, from Le Gros' ruffians, and in doing so averts Rosamond's abduction and becomes acquainted with her. In both versions Henry and Rosamond are secretly married, but in Miller, Henry was at the time already married to Eleanor, who is later unable to compel her to confess the event, whereas in Egan the marriage to Rosamond is annulled in order that Henry may wed Eleanor, who later fails to extract from her a denial of the secret marriage. In both novels Henry promises to divorce Eleanor and make Rosamond queen if she prefers it. The single abduction episode in Miller is increased to three in Egan. The two children, William and Geoffrey, appear in both versions, and although Egan does not subject William to kidnapping, he follows Miller in making him the object of Eleanor's threat of violence. In both novels Rosamond retires to end her days in Godstow Nunnery, her life spared in Miller because Ugglethred had prepared a harmless potion for her, in Egan by the time arrival of Aldred to slay the Saracen slave and Le Gros and to take the queen prisoner. Both novelists devote a scene to Henry's last view of Rosamond at Godstow Nunnery.

Egan arouses the interest of the reader by gradually increasing the beauty of Rosamond's character in the early pages of his novel, and by increasing the number as well as the cunning of her enemies. From the beginning the two rejected lovers, Prince Eustace, a new historical character in the story, and Le Gros—roles which are dispensed with altogether in the earlier novel—practice their villainy against Rosamond. The threat to her is increased also by Egan's doubling the villains in Eleanor's service by adding to Le Gros a newcomer to the tradition, a Saracen slave, one Saladan.[32] To counteract the work of these knaves, Egan creates a new role in the person of Hubert de St. Clair, the loyal friend of Henry, and makes constant use of the good offices of Aldred, the servant of Rosamond and keeper of the bower, who marries Githa, Rosamond's maid—a pair corresponding to Maud and Vidal in Miller's novel. The repetition by Egan of many of Miller's innovations no doubt helped to establish them firmly in the nineteenth-century tradition, and so explains in part their frequent use later in the century in the drama as well as in the novel and short story.

In 1851 Mrs. Kate Charlotte (Prittie) Maberly, "author of 'Emily,' 'Leontine,' 'Melanthe,' 'Fashion,' etc.," published in London a three-volume historical romance, *The Lady and the Priest*. As the title indicates, interest is directed to the career of Thomas À Becket and his relation to Fair Rosamond. At the opening of the story Father Thomas, as prior of the abbey of Severnstoke in Gloucestershire, at the request of the Lady Isolda of the neighboring convent of Clairvaux, gives advice as to the disciplining of one Lady Rosamond, a headstrong girl of seventeen who is guilty of infraction of minor regulations of the convent. Somewhat later Rosamond's father, Lord de Clifford, who for four years had been in the Holy Land, and had left his daughter with the convent during his absence, returns home very ill. Rosamond, accompanied by her maid Joan and Ranulph de Broc, visits him at Clifford Castle on the Wye. Father Thomas also comes to pray for Lord de Clifford, who fully recovers from his illness. But meantime he has become so dependent upon the sympathy and ministrations of his daughter that he cannot send her back to the convent. Accordingly, she is made "chatelaine of Clifford Castle" and, not for love, but in obedience to her father's wishes, she is affianced to Ranulph de Broc. Soon thereafter King Henry pays a visit to Clifford Castle, and he and Rosamond fall in love with each other. He asks to see Prior Thomas Becket of Severnstoke Abbey, who has been recommended to him by Theobald, Archbishop of Canterbury, and released of some of the vows in

[32] This character may have been suggested to Egan by Agnes Strickland's *Lives of the Queens of England*, the first volume of which had appeared in 1840. See *Lives*, 8 vols. (Philadelphia, 1893), I, 254: "There are letters still extant from Suger, by which it appears that the king [Louis VII] had written to him complaints of the criminal attachment of his queen to a young Saracen emir of great beauty, named Sal-Addin." The reference is to the queen's sojourn in Jerusalem, whither she had accompanied Louis VII on his ill-fated crusade. It should be noted, however, that a similar character, Dwerga the dwarf, is used in George Darley's *Thomas À Becket* (1840). See below, pp. 89-91.

order that he may serve the king. Henry, Becket, and Rosamond ride to the hunt together, and Becket proves his ability as a wise adviser in many ways. Clifford, again planning a pilgrimage to the Holy Land, wishes Rosamond to marry Ranulph. Becket, however, advises him to permit her to use her own judgment in such an important matter. Rosamond thereupon refuses Ranulph, and at Clifford's and Ranulph's departure she is left behind as a ward of the king and queen. She is removed to Woodstock Palace, where Henry delighted to reside (though Queen Eleanor spent most of her time in France), and Beatrix de Castro, a favorite of the queen, is chosen as her companion. Now, both Beatrix and the queen are in love with Count Etienne de Blois. Henry's confession of love to Rosamond has prompted her to think of quitting the court to enter Godstow Nunnery, and she is shocked to learn from Becket that Henry has decided to give her in marriage to Count Etienne—a decision which infuriates the queen against Rosamond. When Henry again protests his love, Rosamond refuses to marry the count and abandons any idea of entering Godstow. When she later confesses to Becket that she has been seduced by Henry, he reproaches her bitterly for her sin, and compels her to bequeath all her possessions to the church. Two years pass, Becket is living in splendor as archbishop of Canterbury, and Rosamond has borne two children by Henry. She writes to Becket that her father is returning from the Holy Land, and Becket, worried lest civil war may ensue from Clifford's discovery of the king's treatment of Rosamond, rides posthaste to Woodstock and offers her sanctuary in holy Church. At the same time he shocks her by vehemently declaring that he loves her and is powerless to subdue his passion. She refuses him, saying her love of him has never been more than a daughter's love. Later, at a service in Canterbury Cathedral, attended by Lord de Clifford and Ranulph, Becket excommunicates with three other persons "Rosamond de Clifford, of Clifford Castle in Herefordshire, convicted of having by her counsels urged on the king in open rebellion against the holy see." Rosamond, now at Godstow, learns of Becket's action, and persuades the abbess to seek Henry's help in France. She returns to Woodstock Palace to find that Hubert, the caretaker, has been murdered, and she is told that the children have been abducted by Edward Grimm, Becket's secretary, and other priests in soldier's cloaks. Ranulph de Broc appears before her and offers to see the king, and when he hears of Becket's treatment of Rosamond, he vows vengeance against the priest. Again he asks her to marry him, but she refuses as being unworthy of him. In time, worry about her children and other difficulties temporarily deranges Rosamond's mind. Becket and Eleanor in disguise visit her at Woodstock, but the shock of Rosamond's recognition of Becket restores her to sanity. Becket, who has served Eleanor well, and has given her Henry's letters to Rosamond, now plots with her to make young Henry king, and so to gain complete sway of the empire. Rosamond visits her home, but Clifford refuses to see her, and all the servants flee in fear from the excommunicate. Accompanied by Joan, her faithful maid, she rides to Clairvaux Convent, where later the king and Ranulph find her on her deathbed. She asks forgiveness for Becket and dies. Ranulph de Broc, accompanied by Fitzurse, de Morville, Tracy, and Brito, ride to Canterbury, where they murder Becket in the cathedral. When the deed is done, Ranulph cries, "Rosamond, thou art avenged! I have fulfilled my vow!"

It is clear that Mrs. Maberly gives much more than usual prominence to Thomas À Becket, and, possibly taking a cue from Thomas Miller's *Fair Rosamond* (1839), brings him into greater intimacy with Fair Rosamond than any of her predecessors had dared to do. Actually he is the traditional rival lover, who, upon being rejected by his lady, turns absolute villain and takes his revenge upon her.[33] As Mrs. Maberly portrays him, he is a strong, shrewd, ambitious character who falls violently in love with Rosamond, but, failing to win her, avenges the slight by depriving her of her possessions, excommunicating her, and driving her temporarily insane. Moreover, by joining in conspiracy with Queen Eleanor to incite young Henry to rebellion against his father he becomes not merely the traditional villainous agent of the queen, nor even the Becket of Ireland's *Henry the Second* (1799),[34] who wished merely to get even with his royal enemy. He is rather an unscrupulous man of unquenchable ambition who would stop at nothing to win control of the empire. For such a character Mrs. Maberly devised a tragic end, one that is both unhistorical and untraditional. He is not martyred because Henry's knights think the king can no longer brook the proud prelate's opposition, and so wishes him out of the way. He is slain because the true but unsuccessful lover of Rosamond, Ranulph de Broc, has vowed that the villainous priest should pay with his life for the wrongs he has inflicted upon Fair Rosamond. This same Ranulph de Broc begins in the traditional role of the rival lover, the conventional and paternally approved fiancé supplanted by the king—a well-known figure in the chapbooks—[35] but, unlike any earlier character of the kind, he loves on to the end, and avenges his sweetheart's sufferings by the murder of her oppressor.

In addition to these significant variations upon features already in the literary tradition, some minor borrowings need to be noticed. Mrs.

[33] See Leicester in Hawkins's *Henry and Rosamond* (1749), below, pp. 75-7; Raymond De Burgh in Barnett, below, pp. 88-9; and D'Agneville, above, pp. 47-8.

[34] See below, pp. 79-82.

[35] See Lord Fitzwalters, above, pp. 40ff.

Maberly probably takes a hint from Pierce Egan's novel when she transfers the name Hubert from Henry's loyal friend to his caretaker at Woodstock Palace. From him, too, or from his immediate predecessor, Thomas Miller, she may have derived the abduction of William and Geoffrey. From Miller she very likely drew her notion of Lord Clifford's pilgrimages to the Holy Land. On the other hand, a certain number of traditional or recently common elements of the story are not used. The secret marriage, for example, which had been prominent in recent versions, is not employed, nor is any labyrinth or maze provided by which Rosamond may be safeguarded against surprise. Although the queen is suspicious of Henry's attentions to Rosamond, she does not plot her death. Any evil designs she may have had are never brought to execution because of Rosamond's temporary insanity and her later retirement to the convent to die.

In view of the appearance of successive editions of chapbooks throughout England and of the three ambitious novels just noticed, it is not surprising to recall that in 1854 Charles Dickens should have taken some notice of the "pretty story" of Rosamond in his *Child's History of England,*[36] though he appends to his version of the tale a corrective comment for the benefit of his young readers of history: "Now," he says, "there *was* a fair Rosamond, and she was (I dare say) the loveliest girl in all the world, and the king was certainly very fond of her, and the bad Queen Eleanor was certainly made jealous. But I am afraid—I say afraid, because I like the story so much—that there was no bower, no labyrinth, no silken clue, no dagger, no poison. I am afraid Fair Rosamond retired to a nunnery near Oxford, and died there, peaceably; her sister-nuns hanging a sliken drapery over her tomb, and often dressing it with flowers, in remembrance of the youth and beauty that had enchanted the king when he too was young, and when his life lay fair before him."

Another indication of the popularity of the story in the middle of the century is to be seen in the fact that it makes up a considerable portion of the life of "Eleanor of Aquitaine" in *Romantic Incidents in the Lives of the Queens of England,* by John Frederick Smith, "author of 'Stanfield Hall,' 'Amy Lawrence,' etc."[37] Smith's story deserves some brief notice because of certain untraditional features it contains. Henry

[36] *Works,* Nonesuch ed., 25 vols. (London, 1937-8), I, 545.

[37] New York, 1853, pp. 157-66. The title-page of this edition erroneously prints the author's name as "J. P. Smith, Esq.," and similar errors are made in reprints of his other works in America (see O. A. Roorbach, *Bibliotheca Americana* [from 1820 to 1852], p. 506, where *Amy Lawrence* is assigned to "T. P. Smith"). John Frederick Smith was a prolific popular writer. For comment on him, see *The Athenaeum* for March 15, 1890, p. 343; *The Quarterly Review,* CLXXI (1890), pp. 162-4; Henry Vizetelly, *Glances back through Seventy Years* (London, 1893), II, 12-13. I have not found record of an earlier edition of *Romantic Incidents,*

met Rosamond, we are told, on his first visit to England late in King Stephen's reign. "The poor girl had been deluded by her royal lover from her home under pretence of marriage, which a mock priest had celebrated between them. Reasons of state alone, Henry had stated, prevented his acknowledging her openly as his queen. In the confidence of her loving heart, she trusted to him, and was deceived" (p. 159). She had two children by him, but later he married Eleanor of Aquitaine and upon King Stephen's death became king of England. One day, as Eleanor was sitting in her apartment at Oxford, her suspicion of Henry was aroused when she observed "a ball of silk which had been caught in one of his spurs. As silk at that time was only worn by persons of most exalted rank, she naturally wondered in whose society her husband could have been." She followed him to Woodstock, and, penetrating "into the depths of the woods, she soon discovered a door artfully hid in a maze." She entered to find Rosamond seated by a cradle in which an infant was slumbering. Temporarily angered because Rosamond thought her to be Henry's mother, the Empress Maude, she at the same time remembered her own frailties" and realized that Rosamond had been victimized by Henry and by circumstances. She persuaded Rosamond to promise never to see Henry again and to enter a nunnery, and she in turn gave her word that the children would be properly cared for. Then follow a detailed description of the ceremony at Godstow, at which Rosamond became a nun, and an account of how King Henry entered at the conclusion of the rites to demand that Rosamond should be returned to him; and how he was checked in his violence only by the swift and firm intervention of the prelate in charge; whereupon Rosamond swooned and was borne away, and Henry, as he left, ordered the imprisonment of Eleanor.

Here for the first time Henry arranges a marriage by a "mock priest," and is presented as an unscrupulous deceiver. The device of the "ball of silk" caught in his spur had been used by no author since Holinshed.[38] Perhaps Smith's most surprising departure from tradition is that the queen comes to Rosamond, not armed with dagger and poison and fired by the passions of jealousy and revenge, but offering sympathy and understanding to a king's unfortunate victim, and intent upon using her powers of persuasion to set all to rights. This complete reversal of the queen's character is traceable, of course, to Thomas Hull's *Henry the Second* (1774).[39] Rosamond's retirement to Godstow had by

and the Library of Congress can locate only two other copies in America—one in the Grosvenor Library in Buffalo and one in the New York Public Library, dated 1854. The copy from which I quote is in Deering Library of Northwestern University. For the facts above I am indebted to Mr. Robert C. Gooch, Chief, General Reference and Bibliography Division, Library of Congress.

[38] See above, p. 11.

[39] See below, pp. 77-9.

this time become quite common since the time of Addison, but the account of the scene created by the king when Rosamond was taking her vows has not been met with before.

Following the rather considerable display of interest in the Rosamond story by writers of prose fiction during the middle years of the century, no further prose version made its appearance, so far as I know, until 1910, when Bernard Capes included one in his collection of *Historical Vignettes.*[40] Despite its brevity it reveals some striking variations on earlier motifs. The first of these occurs at the opening of the story, where Eleanor, accompanied by a knight named De Polewarth, forces a churl, apparently a servant belonging to Woodstock Manor, to point out to her the garden containing the secret bower. Again, to show Eleanor's cruel nature, Capes makes her stab little William's white rabbit with her bodkin, for no apparent reason at all, and proceed on her way as if what she had done had been only a trifling matter in her day's routine. This, no doubt, is but a logical extension of her uncalled-for attempt to stab young William, as recounted in Thomas Miller's *Fair Rosamond* (1839),[41] or of her threat to kill young Geoffrey in his cradle, according to Pierce Egan's version,[42] or of her impulse to commit a similar act in Winspere's *Fair Rosamond* (1882).[43] We are told, too, that quite by accident she comes upon "the end of a strong green thread hanging out of the darkness" of the forest, and by following it is brought into the garden, where she comes face-to-face with Rosamond. The labyrinth itself is described in more than ordinary detail:

> Stepping to a birch-tree, [she] parted the green and disappeared. It was a cunning blind, as she had expected. The great trunk was so packed amongst the thickets of the hillside that none would have guessed its concealment of a scarce-discernible track which threaded the matted growths above and behind it. Mounting by this, the malign creature came suddenly upon a broken opening in the rock, so mossy and so choked with foliage that its presence would have been quite unsuspected from the glade below. . . . Looped over a projection of the stone, was the end of a strong green thread hanging out of the darkness. . . . The cavity led into a ramification of passages, roughly trenched and hewn out of the calcareous slate of the hill. Occasionally roofed, mostly open, always tangled in foliage, and so cunningly devised to mislead that it had been near humanly impossible to resolve its intricacies without such a guide to follow, the labyrinth led the Queen by a complicated course to a sense of approaching light and release. And then all in a moment the thread had come to an end against a stake to which it was fastened;

[40] London, 1910, pp. 185-95.
[41] See above, p. 51.
[42] See above, p. 55.
[43] See below, p. 105.

> and there was a pleasant garden sunk in a hollow of a hill, and a fair young woman, with an awaiting, somewhat troubled expression on her face, standing hard by. She had evidently spun the clue, and returned the first by it from the glade, to make sport for her little man.[44]

Few authors, especially in such a briefly-told tale, have given so detailed an account of one of the most interesting features of the legend. Threatened with the dagger, Rosamond is compelled to drink poison, but just before she dies, the queen informs her that her young William had "betrayed the way" to her, and tries to leave the impression that he had been put to death—another indication of the queen's cruel nature. This idea may have been suggested to Capes by George Darley's *Becket* (1840), in which Eleanor sought without success to get the secret of the bower from her own son Richard, who had informed her that while playing about the manor he had seen the Fairy Queen;[45] but perhaps it bears a closer resemblance to Tennyson's use of little Geoffrey, who, thinking Eleanor was the queen of the fairies, actually conducted her to his mother.[46]

The story of Rosamond has an important part in Clara Turnbull's novel, *The Damsel Dark*,[47] which relates the adventures of one Fredègonda of Tournoir Castle, a female knight known as the Damsel Dark or the Knight of the Woods, and of her love for Sir Etienne of Estorel. As an adherent of the Empress Maud, Fredègonda befriends Rosamond, who with babe in arms is being pursued by jealous Queen Eleanor, whose violence against her even before the altar of the church is prevented only by the quick action of Becket. Although Rosamond's marriage to Henry antedates Eleanor's, she resolves to renounce her claims to recognition in order to save England from civil war. Attempting to retire to a convent, she and her babe are overtaken and imprisoned by Eleanor, who leaves her a dagger and poison. Fredègonda rescues her and conducts her to Godstow Nunnery. At London, Eleanor's attempt to persuade Henry that the Knight of the Woods (Fredègonda, whom, of course, she thinks a male knight) is in love with Rosamond fails completely when Fredègonda reveals herself as a woman. Henry learns from Fredègonda all the unhappiness that Eleanor has brought to Rosamond. Later, Prince Eustace and his villainous followers seize Fredègonda and Rosamond, and upon hearing that they are to be forced into marriage, Henry and a band of retainers rescue them at the Abbey of St. Edmond. Fredègonda marries Sir Etienne, and Henry rides away with Rosamond.

[44] Pp. 191-2.
[45] See below, p. 90.
[46] See below, p. 110.
[47] London, 1912.

As a concurrent but subsidiary episode in the novel, the Rosamond story is of necessity not told in its entirety. But most of the chief elements of the author's conception of the legend are clear. Henry's legal marriage to Rosamond on an earlier visit to England clearly antedates his union with Eleanor. Rosamond is portrayed as a noble and generous person who has become so unhappy as a result of her undeserved misfortunes that she has resolved to renounce the world and enter a cloister. Pursued by the angry queen who twice uses violence against her, she retires to Godstow, only to be seized by Eustace and his ruffians and rescued by Henry. Presumably, since she again succumbs to her love for strong-willed Henry, she does not return to Godstow, but the author gives no indication of what was to be her fate. In fact, her entanglement in the love-triangle at the end of the story is exactly as it had been at the beginning. The general influence of Pierce Egan's *Fair Rosamond* (1844) may be detected in the character of the action, and specifically in Rosamond's decision to relinquish her claims upon Henry and to retire to the convent, as well as in the use of Prince Eustace and his followers. The minor role of Becket as Rosamond's protector against Eleanor's violence was well established in nineteenth-century tradition. Becket's prevention of the queen's stabbing of Rosamond, however, may have been suggested by Tennyson's play.[48]

What is apparently a similar type of novel is Dorothy Brandon's *Beau Regard*,[49] characterized by Jonathan Nield as "A rather sensational Troubadour story, dealing with the time of Becket and Fair Rosamond," into which "Queen Eleanor . . . is prominently introduced."[50] To what extent the story of Rosamond figures in the plot, I cannot say, because I have not been able to see a copy of the work.

E. Barrington (Mrs. Lilly Adams Beck, née Moresby), in her short tale, "The King and the Lady," published in 1924,[51] reports the story as told by "Dame Petronille, woman formerly to Eleanor, Queen of Henry Fitz-Empress, the Second Henry of England," and recorded by "the holy Canon of the Chapel of St. Nicholas."[52] She tells how Henry had met and wedded Rosamond before he married Eleanor of Aquitaine, and how the queen became suspicious of her from their first meeting at the English court. Fair Rosamond, who was fully conscious of her embarrassing situation, paled, became ill, and expressed the wish to return to her home. But Eleanor refuses her request and attempts to

[48] See below, p. 110

[49] London, 1920.

[50] *Guide to the Best Historical Novels and Tales* (New York, 1929), no. 273.

[51] In *The Gallants Following according to Their Wont the Ladies!* (Boston [1924]), pp. 3-30.

[52] The name Petronille was probably suggested by Petronilla, one of the names applied to the sister of Eleanor. See Agnes Strickland, *Lives*, I, 248, note.

keep her in seclusion from the king. Nurse Petronille convinces the queen that if she may be allowed to guard Rosamond, she will act as a spy upon the pair. Instead, she actually dedicates herself to the service of the lovers. By carrying Rosamond's ring to Henry as a token that she is in need of him, Petronille arranges a meeting, at which Henry learns that Rosamond has no wish to be queen, but does fear for the future of her unborn child. Accordingly, he places her in a maze at Woodstock with Petronille (who has led the queen to believe that she is going back to Aquitaine) as her nurse, and Simon of Winchester as keeper of the bower. There, in due time, young William is born. Later, we are told, after one of Henry's visits to Rosamond, Petronille notices a ball of "broidering silk" tangled about his spur. One afternoon, Eleanor appears at the entrance to the bower, and Petronille, in warning Rosamond and seeking to bar the intruder's way, is wounded by her dagger. Face to face with the queen, Rosamond refuses to swear to give up Henry, and in vain she pleads that she may be spared for her son's sake and be permitted to retire to Godstow Nunnery. Eleanor is unrelenting, and Rosamond, refusing the dagger, drinks the poison and dies. The queen smiles and leaves. Rosamond's body is placed in a tomb at Godstow with the usual epitaph inscribed upon it.

Petronille will be recognized as a variation upon the well-known character of Alethea of the chapbooks. Although she does not, like Alethea, lend aid to the seduction of Rosamond, which had taken place sometime before, she is an agent in promoting the illicit love affair. The untraditional feature of her role is that she plays false to her mistress, the queen, in order to serve the lovers. The stabbing of Rosamond's nurse has not been used by any earlier writer. Rosamond's residence at court, Simon of Winchester as keeper of the bower, the birth of young William, the thread caught in the king's spur, the manner of Rosamond's death, and her burial at Godstow—all these components of the story are so well known as to need no documentation.

In E. O. Browne's *Fair Rosamond*[53] the reader's interest is converged upon the rivalry of Henry, Duke of Anjou, later King Henry II of England, and of his loyal friend Sir Richard de Gifford, for the love of Rosamond de Clifford. Sir Richard meets her at a religious house on the Severn, and is so smitten with love of her that he immediately proposes marriage. Her father, the gruff, cruel Baron Walter de Clifford, refuses, and Sir Richard leaves the abbey. Soon thereafter Henry, fleeing from Prince Eustace's men and taking refuge in the same house, is compelled to hide in Rosamond's chamber while the place is being searched. He falls in love with her and introduces himself as his own non-existent half-brother. When de Clifford accuses Rosamond of

[53] London [1932].

wantonness, Henry defends her and compels a cowled figure whom he discovers under the table to marry them forthwith. The next day, upon learning that the performer of the ceremony is one of Prince Eustace's soldiers in disguise, Henry slays him. He now knows that his marriage to Rosamond is unlawful. After separate return visits to Rosamond, Henry as her husband and Sir Richard as her hopeful but unencouraged lover, the two friends spend some time in France. Upon his return to England, Sir Richard again seeks to win Rosamond (who, meantime, unknown to him, has given birth to a son, Geofrey). De Clifford's attempt to trick him into marriage to Rosamond's sister fails. Henry, now married to Eleanor of Aquitaine, returns to England and accidentally meets Rosamond and her child, who have been so mistreated by de Clifford that they have fled his home. Still believing him to be his own half-brother, Rosamond gives Henry a girdle embroidered with roses and broom. Later, recognizing the girdle, Sir Richard knows that she has become Henry's mistress. Henry provides her with every luxury, surrounding her with her old nurse Malkin, a page, and a guard of loyal soldiers. During another of Henry's absences in France she gives birth to a second son, William. After the death of King Stephen, Henry and Eleanor return to England as king and queen. Henry now reveals his true identity to Walter de Clifford, gives him lands in Shropshire, exacts his homage, and tells him that Rosamond is henceforth to be under royal protection. She, in turn, is informed that she must keep close and not attend the coronation ceremonies lest the king himself should fall in love with her. Henry presents little Geoffrey to Queen Eleanor, but refuses to reveal the identity of the mother, and places him in the care of Thomas Becket. Meantime he has had Hugh de Morville, architect of the royal palace, prepare a labyrinth and manor house for Rosamond in Woodstock Park. Eleanor's suspicions grow to positive jealousy, and she unsuccessfully tries to obtain from Rosamond's young William some information about his mother and her place of residence. She is further aroused by noticing a thread of silk caught in Henry's spur. She resolves upon bold action. Suggesting to Sir Richard that a secret door to the labyrinth is the work of the king's enemies, she prevails upon him to break it down. By following the silken clue they come upon Rosamond. In a dramatic scene which follows, Rosamond learns for the first time that her lover-husband is not the king's half-brother, but the king himself. Eleanor is prevented by Sir Richard from stabbing her rival, and, thinking Rosamond will elope with the knight, she leaves them together in the bower. But Rosamond persuades Sir Richard to take her to Godstow Nunnery, where she takes the veil. For these acts Sir Richard is imprisoned by the king, but is soon thereafter released upon a moving plea from his wife, Isabel; and, after Henry has explained his position from the beginning, the two friends are reconciled.

This work is a significant version of the story with which to close this chapter, because the attempt on the part of authors since the eighteenth century to adhere with increasing faithfulness to the historical elements in the story, finds its most acceptable result in Browne's *Fair Rosamond.* The list of characters, designated as historical and imaginary, which he prefixes to his novel, suggests that he is conscious of a self-imposed obligation—that he wishes to remind the reader that his story has not been written without regard for historical fact. Even though the marriage of Henry and Rosamond is sudden and forced—though perhaps plausible enough in such troubled times—and the maintenance of Henry's disguise over a number of years may be a *tour de force,* still they create a situation which plausibly and logically enough leads to events which are historical. Moreover, in assigning to Becket a very minor role and in never once involving him in the love affair, Browne has discarded an attractive but extravagant invention of the nineteenth century in favor of historical probability. Finally, Rosamond's retirement to Godstow Nunnery, which is a matter of historical record, is not here a result of Eleanor's violence, but of the discovery of Henry's true identity and of the illegality of her marriage—compelling motives both. Historical also are the granting of lands in Shropshire to Baron Walter de Clifford, and Browne's rejection of any punishment of Eleanor for her part in the affair of Rosamond and Henry; for, as has been pointed out before, it is highly improbable that as a close prisoner she could have had an opportunity to perform any of the acts against Rosamond which tradition has persisted in laying to her charge.

On the other hand, the author has made use of a number of traditional elements, both early and late in origin, and has, of course, freely invented such other characters and situations as were needed to give body and variety to his story. Some of the oldest components of the legend still survive in the reference to the silk caught in Henry's spur, and in the use of the rival lover, of Nurse Malkin, and of the labyrinth, here constructed specifically for Rosamond by Henry's architect, Hugh de Morville. In his elaboration of the difficulties which the queen experiences in ascertaining Rosamond's identity and her place of residence, and in actually reaching her in the bower, Browne is following a practice developed in such late authors as George Darley, Pierce Egan, Tennyson, and Capes. But he is probably more successful than his predecessors in rendering Rosamond's place of seclusion historically acceptable. Other features of the same recent origin are the two children, Geoffrey and William; the questioning of the latter by Eleanor as to his mother's place of residence, and her cruelty in having him whipped;[54] Prince Eustace as a leader of a band of ruffians;[55] Baron Walter de Clifford,[56] who is here made cruel, uncouth, and unscrupulous; and the secret marriage—a nineteenth-century development. In the matter of the secret marriage and of Henry's disguise of his identity, however, Browne's version differs from all others in that both are begun in good faith and maintained in secrecy to the end, with results which alter the entire plot of the novel.[57]

The beautiful loyalty of Sir Richard Gifford to King Henry, transcending as it does his love of Rosamond, is one of the most attractive inventions in Browne's novel. In him are fused two ordinarily incompatible characters found in the nineteenth-century tradition—the rejected rival lover, represented, for example, by Mrs. Maberly's Ranulph de Broc, and the faithful friend of the king, best portrayed in Egan's Hubert de St. Clair.[58] It is ironic enough that Sir Richard, in loyalty to his liege, is compelled to keep from the woman he loves the damaging secrets of his friend; it is more ironic still that in all innocence he becomes an agent of the jealous queen in her schemes against them both, is forced to witness his beloved's humiliation and shame, and at her request to perform the unpleasant duty of conducting her to sanctuary in Godstow Nunnery. These relationships among the characters of the novel lead to a denouement unlike any other of the many ingenious ones which relieve Queen Eleanor of her traditional role as the murderess of Fair Rosamond.

It may be concluded that the Rosamond story attained a rather late development in prose fiction. It is true, of course, that the chapbook version with its fairly complicated plot was in the hands of readers as early as 1640, but nothing more elaborate appeared until the publication of Thomas Miller's *Fair Rosamond* in 1839, Pierce Egan's *Fair Rosamond* in 1844, and Mrs. Maberly's *The Lady and the Priest* in 1851. These long historical romances were evidently inspired by the interest in feudal times aroused by the success of Sir Walter Scott's novels. It is hardly surprising that lengthy novels on the Rosamond story did not continue to appear at regular intervals; but that several

[54] See above, p. 61, and below, pp. 119-20.

[55] See above, pp. 53ff., 62ff.

[56] Who first appears as a character in the chapbooks of the seventeenth century, and undergoes various transformations in the next two centuries. See above, pp. 40ff., 50ff., 56ff., and below, pp. 75-6, 78, 89-90.

[57] But the maintenance of the king's disguise should be compared with his disguise as Edgar, the troubadour, in Barnett's opera, below, p. 88. But cf. also Eleanor's disclosure to Rosamond of the priority of her own marriage to Henry, in Winspere's *Fair Rosamond* (1882), III, iv; and below, pp. 104ff.

[58] See above, pp. 56ff., 53ff.

short tales or short-stories and three full-length novels have been written on the subject in the present century is some indication that the theme has not lost its attraction for writers of prose fiction. By its very nature the novel developed a number of new characters and situations, and multiplied variations on old motifs—all of which helped greatly to enrich the tradition. Probably it contributed more to dramatic versions written in the past hundred years than the earlier drama had contributed to it. The novelist demonstrated, for example, what uses could be made of the children of Henry and Rosamond, and of such devices as disguise, abduction, elopement, raids, secrecy, and variations on the marriage-theme. But the dramatist had concerned himself with the story long before it was looked upon seriously by the novelist, and, as the rest of this study will attempt to show, the Rosamond story attained its greatest popularity on the stage.

CHAPTER IV

THE DRAMA: 1693-1840

WHY A STORY which had had its first literary success among the poets of the Age of Elizabeth should never have been made the subject of a full-length play by any of the dramatists of the time is a question that can be answered only by conjecture.[1] Indeed, no such treatment was accorded the story until a full century after the first appearance of a literary version of it. John Bancroft's *Henry the Second, King of England; with the Death of Rosamond,* which was acted at the Theatre Royal in 1692, was published in London the next year with a Prologue by Will: Mountfort[2] and an epilogue by John Dryden. Following a common practice of Restoration dramatists where moral lapses are involved, both authors express a flippant attitude toward Rosamond's indiscretion. Mountfort declares that

> though she fell by Jealous Cruelty,
> For Venial Sin 'twas pity she should die.
> Ah! should your Wives and Daughters be so try'd,
> And with her Dose their Failings purify'd,
> Lord! What a Massacre wou'd mawl Cheapside![3]

John Genest comments that "the original story of Rosamond did not furnish material for five acts—the author of this T. was therefore obliged

[1] The poisoning of Fair Rosamond by one Skinke, and the imprisonment of the queen are discussed in *Look about You* (1600), but Rosamond does not herself appear in the play. See above, pp. 23-4. In his *Dictionary of Old English Plays* (London, 1860), p. 91, J. O. Halliwell suggests that, from mention of Fair Rosamond in an old song on Bartholomew Fair, it may be conjectured that a droll was acted there in the seventeenth century. On September 9, 1653, Henry Moseley entered in the Stationers' Register (Eyre, i, 428) among other plays a "Hen: the 2d. by Shakespeare and Davenport," and Warburton's list of plays destroyed by fire contains a "Henry ye 1st" by the same authors. (See Chambers, *The Elizabethan Stage,* III, 489.) But nothing more is known of either play. If a play on Henry II ever existed, it is very likely, in view of a very considerable contemporary interest in the story, that it made some use of the Rosamond theme.

[2] Although the play appeared among Mountfort's plays in 1720, it is generally assigned to Bancroft. As Joseph Knight (DNB., sub "Bancroft") points out, the Prologue signed by Mountfort bears a date subsequent to his murder. See also Montague Summers, *A Bibliography of Restoration Drama* (London [1934]), p. 22.

[3] Cf. Dryden, ll. 7-16 (*Poems,* ed. John Sergeant, London, 1913, p. 258). Curiously enough, Dryden asserts that "*Jane Clifford* was her Name, as Books aver:/ Fair *Rosamond* was but her *Nom de Guerre*" (ll. 5-6). I know of no other instance in which the name Jane is applied to her. Perhaps Dryden was being facetious.

to make additions to it."[4] Some of these "additions," which became a permanent part of the tradition, give the play more historic than intrinsic importance—though it must be said in all fairness that it is not without merit as a historical tragedy. The major addition (not used before), which complicates the plot, perhaps unduly, is the use of the struggle between Henry and the Church as represented by the Abbot, who is an enemy of the king on Becket's account, and by the priest Bertrard, Rosamond's confessor, who becomes the tool of the Abbot to effect his foul scheme.

Omitting characters who are introduced primarily to expand the political situation involved, we may outline the story as follows: Sir Thomas Vaughan, the king's favorite and, by his own admission, actually "the King's pimp," can make no progress in furthering Henry's suit to Rosamond, and the king himself is much discomfited by her obstinacy. At the moment when Rosamond's Woman is steadfastly refusing to allow Sir Thomas to see her, the king enters and by his persuasive wooing so weakens her resistance that she eventually succumbs to his will. The Abbot, who is plotting to stir up rebellion against the king and set up young Henry in his stead, having learned from the priest Bertrard, Rosamond's confessor, of the king's illicit love, informs the queen of the affair. She commands Bertrard to lead them to Rosamond, and, appearing with the Abbot before her rival, she is prevented from stabbing her only by the sudden arrival of the king and Verulam. To placate her, the king swears that his feeling for Rosamond was but a passing infatuation now already gone, and it is Eleanor whom he really loves. The Abbot, secretly bemoaning the apparent reconciliation of the king and queen, encourages Henry to hope that he may be able to win back Rosamond, now convinced of his falseness, by promising to divorce the queen. Gloating over his triumph, the Abbot incenses Eleanor by informing her that the king plans to divorce her and to deprive her sons of their rights. He advises her to poison Rosamond on the morrow, and promises that Bertrard will lead them to the place of concealment at Woodstock. Meantime, the king, who must go to France to put down the rebellion raised by his son, takes leave of Rosamond, who tells him of an evil dream that has made her fear the queen, and begs in vain that she may accompany him as his page. Upon a pretext that the queen wishes to ask Rosamond's pardon for her abuse of her, Bertrard is persuaded, by promise of advancement, to lead the queen and her party to Rosamond's Bower. Bertrard, accompanied by his band of villains, and pretending he has "A Message from the King, and a Present for the Lady," tricks Sir Thomas Vaughan to gain admission, and then stabs him. The king,

[4] *Some Account of the English Stage from the Restoration in 1660 to 1830,* 10 vols. (Bath, 1832), II, 27-8.

who had been warned in a dream of Rosamond's death in flames fed by Eleanor, comes to the bower, and learns from Sir Thomas what has happened. Meantime the queen, warned of the king's approach, offers Rosamond the choice of a dagger or a cup of poison. She drinks the poison just before the king enters with Verulam, and she dies in his arms. Bertrard dies of poisoned wine which he has innocently imbibed, Sir Thomas mortally wounds the Abbot and dies, and the king dismisses the queen but swears that he will be avenged by punishing her and her treacherous son.

Bancroft had read Daniel, Drayton, Deloney, and possibly the chapbook version of his day; but he displays some ingenuity in his departures from and additions to them. For example, Warner's "Knight of trust," who was Drayton's Vaughan and Deloney's Sir Thomas, becomes in Bancroft, by a simple process of addition, Sir Thomas Vaughan—with, however, a rather important function added to his office as keeper of the labyrinth at Woodstock. The role of go-between (represented in Daniel as a "seeming Matron," in Drayton as a "wicked woman," and in Thomas May as "an ancient Dame") is by Bancroft assigned to Sir Thomas, and Rosamond's Woman becomes the true guardian of her virtue.[5] Bancroft gives very little attention to the physical scene of his play, but he seems to follow Daniel, or possibly Thomas May, in assigning the seduction of Rosamond to a place other than the bower at Woodstock, and to a date prior to her residence there. For his brief reference to the labyrinth (p. 42) he is indebted to Drayton,[6] as his phrasing indicates. Rosamond's expressed desire to accompany Henry to France as his page is an expansion of Deloney, but the dream which warned her of evil to come:

> "Oh! I shall never see thy Face again!
> An evil Dream this Morning entertain'd me,
> And now it is confirm'd." (p. 42)

is new in the tradition, reminding one, perhaps because of the association of the dream and the female page, of the subject of Donne's Elegy XVI, "Of His Mistress."[7]

On the other hand, Bancroft creates new characters and introduces

[5] For discussion of the authors mentioned, see above, pp. 14-27, *passim;* and pp. 40ff. The exchange of roles between the keeper and the procuress may have been suggested to Bancroft by the revival of the story of *Troilus* by Dryden. See Allerdyce Nicoll, *History of Restoration Drama: 1660-1700* (Cambridge, 1923), p. 159: "The satire of priests and the person of Sir Thomas Vaughan, a kind of replica of Pandarus, recall to us *Troilus and Cressida* of Dryden."

[6] See "Henry to Rosamond," ll. 179-80.

[7] For an actual instance of this arrangement between lovers, see Grierson's *Poems of John Donne,* 2 vols. (Oxford, 1912), II, 86. For a later use of this combination, see above, p. 45.

an additional complication of plot into his play by making the collusion of Becket's ecclesiastical partisans and the queen the cause of Rosamond's death. She becomes the pawn for high stakes. Moreover, Bancroft is the first to use the scene in which the queen is foiled in an earlier attempt upon Rosamond's life. The use of Rosamond's confessor to trick Sir Thomas Vaughan, the keeper, by pretending to deliver a message and a present from the king is an extension of the chapbook version, in which the keeper is merely overpowered. Probably an original invention also is Eleanor's offering her victim a choice between a dagger and a cup of poison.[8]—a significant change, because, although Fair Rosamond, despite the attempts made upon her, is never in any version actually stabbed, still in no tragic version subsequent to Bancroft's play is she ever denied a choice between the two lethal instruments. Both Rosamond's evil dream and Henry's warning by dream of her danger—devices not found earlier in the story—may have been inspired by the extraordinary interest of the seventeenth century in dreams in general. Henry says of his dream:

> I cannot rest, some Devils haunt my Soul:
> When late last Night I sunk to my repose,
> A dreadful Vision entertain'd my slumber;
> Poor *Rosamond* methought was all on fire,
> And as I strove to quench the raging object,
> The Queen threw Oyl on the expiring Flames,
> And made 'em blaze a-fresh with fiercer fury." (p. 46)

Since drama imposes upon its author the necessity of providing conflict, a variety of action, and some interest in every important scene, Bancroft introduces new features characterized by some ingenuity. These, as we shall see, mark the beginning of a new development toward greater freedom both in the alteration of the traditional features of the play and in the invention of new ones.

Such possibilities for alteration and expansion of the story were apparently fully grasped by Joseph Addison, for by innovations introduced in his opera *Rosamond* the nature of the traditional story was altered in two directions—toward a tragicomic conception which spares the heroine from death at the hands of Eleanor, and toward burlesque of the entire theme, a form of amusement that was to be much employed in the more popular theatres of the next century. His *Rosamond*.

[8] Unless editions of the chapbook, *The Life and Death of Fair Rosamond,* which antedate Bancroft's play, like the later ones, represent Eleanor as offering Rosamond the alternative of death by the sword. The wording of the chapbook, however, does not indicate that the queen actually brandishes a sword before Rosamond: "she gave her the choice either to drink the cup of poison she had prepared for her, or die by the sword." For a discussion of the oldest chapbook version, see above, p. 40.

An Opera, which was printed twice in 1707 and again in 1713, met with a cold reception at its performance on April 6, 1706, and was soon withdrawn.[9] It is written in three acts and presents seven characters: King Henry, Sir Trusty (keeper of the bower), a Page, a Messenger, Queen Eleanor, Rosamond, and Grideline (wife to Sir Trusty). The entire action takes place at Woodstock Park. As the opera begins, Queen Eleanor and her Page are surveying from a distance Rosamond's Bower in the midst of the Park. Her outbursts of jealousy and vows of revenge are intensified when she hears Henry returning from his victories, returning not to her but to her rival, the Fair Rosamond. As the latter sits alone in her bower, impatiently awaiting the king's arrival and bemoaning her sad fate, Henry appears and orders the keeper, Sir Trusty, to guard the gate. After a brief moment with Rosamond, he declares that he is exhausted, and he retires to sleep. Now, Sir Trusty's love of Fair Rosamond has aroused the jealousy of his wife Grideline. Aware of this, Eleanor's page persuades Grideline to open the gate in order that she may catch Trusty and Rosamond "dallying in the Bower." Eleanor, still muttering vengeance, enters "with a Bowl in one hand, and a Dagger in the other." Commanded to make a choice, Rosamond asks for mercy, pleading her youthful impulsiveness and King Henry's charm as responsible for her fall, and begs that she may be spared, to retire from the world and live in "some deep dungeon." Eleanor forces her to drink from the bowl, and orders her body to be taken to a convent, "where the fam'd streams of *Isis* stray," and where the nuns will "due solemnities perform." Sir Trusty, frightened at the scene before him, also drinks from the bowl, and falls. Meantime, as he sleeps in a grotto, Henry has a dream in which "two Angels suppos'd to be the Guardian Spirits of the British Kings in War and in Peace" prophesy the future greatness of Britain, and show him "the glorious pile" of Blenheim Palace ascending on the spot of Rosamond's Bower.[10] Starting from his sleep, and coming upon Eleanor, he suspects that "Rosamond is dead." Being assured that if Rosamond still lived, Henry would abandon her, reform, and love only Eleanor, the queen tells him that what she had administered to Rosamond was but a sleeping-potion:

> The bowl, with drowsie juices fill'd,
> From cold *Egyptian* drugs distill'd,
> In borrow'd death has clos'd her eyes:
> But soon the waking nymph shall rise,

[9] The music for the opera was provided by Thomas Clayton, who had introduced Italian opera at Drury Lane in 1705.

[10] The opera was dedicated to the Duchess of Marlborough, who resided at Blenheim Palace.

And, in a convent plac'd, admire
The cloister'd walls and virgin choire:
With them in songs and hymns divine
The beauteous penitent shall join,
And bid the guilty world adieu.[11]

At this welcome announcement the king expresses his relief, and asks only to live and die with his queen. Sir Trusty, now revived, and Grideline, agreeing to follow the example of their superiors, are reconciled, and hasten to renew their conjugal vows.

Addison departed from the entire legendary tradition by giving to the tragic story, perhaps in deference to the taste and practice of the age, an ending which, if not happy, is certainly not tragic in the dramatic sense.[12] To achieve this, he has provided a sudden, complete, and unconvincing change in the character of Eleanor, so that when the truth comes out that the potion she had administered was innocuous, the spectator or reader is no doubt as much surprised as Henry himself at the sudden turn of events. Moreover, with the low characters, Sir Trusty and Grideline—hardly the kind we should expect to be entrusted with the keeping of the king's beloved—Addison has created an unsatisfying subplot, apparently designed to burlesque the main theme.[13] Sir Trusty, as his name seems to indicate, could have been suggested to Addison by Warner's "Knight of trust," whose love of Rosamond was unrequited,[14] for the combined roles of keeper and rival lover occur in no other earlier version. But it is hardly necessary to assume that Addison had read that obscure Elizabethan. Sir Trusty is undoubtedly a direct descendant of Sir Thomas Vaughan in Bancroft's play, because, like Sir Thomas, he has no illusions about his role "as principal pimp to the mighty King Harry."[15] His wife, Grideline, bears no resemblance to the long line of temptresses who appear in earlier versions, but is created merely to construct a situation in burlesque of the main

[11] *The Miscellaneous Works of Joseph Addison,* ed. A. C. Guthkelch, 2 vols. (London, 1914), I, 326.

[12] In Deloney's ballad (1593?) Rosamond's plea that she be permitted to retire to a convent should be regarded as part of the background of Addison's revolutionary change, though I imagine that his denouement is a result of a desire to avoid tragedy and to yield to the demands for greater historical accuracy. For Deloney, see above, p. 22.

[13] The tendency toward burlesque of the story, hitherto of slow growth, but reaching large proportions in the next century, is evident in Richard Brathwait's *Drunken Barnaby's Four Journeys* (London, 1716), p. 7, which had first appeared in 1638. The Prologue by Will Mountfort and the Epilogue by Dryden to Bancroft's Henry the Second (1693) are also in flippant vein. See also Tom Brown, *Amusements Serious and Comical* (1700), ed. Arthur L. Hayward (London, 1927), p. 319, where Fair Rosamond is reported by Baron Norton from "the grim Tartarian territories" to be serving as "runner to this bawdy coffee-house" and "Queen Eleanor, her mortal enemy, sells sprats, and has her stall in Pluto's stable-yard."

[14] See above, p. 15.

[15] P. 306. Cf. Bancroft, above, pp. 70ff.

plot. The exploitation of Grideline's jealousy to gain admission to the bower is a new device in the tradition. Eleanor's offering a choice of a bowl of poison or a dagger was derived from Bancroft, with the difference that in the latter the potion was not innocuous and the choice in any case was death. Sir Trusty's drinking the potion is reminiscent of the act of a very different character, Bertrard, in Bancroft. Finally, Henry's dream, obviously thrust into the opera to compliment the Marlborough family, though such dreams are a commonplace in dramatic literature, could well have been inspired by Henry's dream of the greatness of Britain's future in Thomas May's *Reigne of Henry the Second* (1633).[16] There is no evidence, therefore, that Addison made use of either Daniel or Drayton, but he may have read the story of Rosamond in Thomas May, and certainly he was well acquainted with the recent play by John Bancroft.

Bancroft's tragedy and Addison's opera were not followed by any dramatic version of the story until 1749, when William Hawkins published his tragedy of *Henry and Rosamond.* In his "Advertisement" Hawkins says the play had been "offered to the Managers of *Drury-Lane* Theatre, who declined accepting it, for Reasons which appeared to the Author to be rather evasive, than satisfactory." Genest thinks that "the managers were afraid (as well they might) that many passages would be applied to the unfortunate difference between George the 2d and the Prince of Wales."[17] A "hasty Alteration" of the play was produced "at the Theatre at *Birmingham*" in the summer of 1761 by Thomas Hull.[18] Hawkins's play consists of five acts, is written in blank verse, imitative of the Elizabethans in its phrasing, and has eleven characters of name: King Henry the Second, the Prince of Wales, the Duke of Cornwall, Lord Clifford, the Earls of Salisbury, Leicester, Winchester, and Surry, Queen Elinor, Rosamond, and Harriana. The scene is laid "in or near Canterbury," presumably in order to enable the king to ride to Becket's shrine without violating dramatic unity.

As the play opens, Leicester, in love with Rosamond and banished from the court, is seeking revenge on Henry by inciting the Prince of Wales to rebellion. Lord Clifford, Rosamond's father, complains to Salisbury that his long service to the king has been repaid by the seduction of his only child, and he plans to trap Leicester, who is misleading young Henry, by counterfeiting a letter from Rosamond making an assignation. When Henry announces to the queen that he cannot love her, she declares she will love him always, but wishes him and Rosamond all happiness. Henry and the prince quarrel, and the latter stalks out. Henry orders the arrest of Leicester. The queen, now alone,

[16] Sig. D3-D6.
[17] V, 370ff.
[18] See Thomas Hull, *Henry the Second* (London, 1774), Preface, p. i.

declares that Providence will one day vindicate her innocence. Lord Clifford, disguised as a begging friar, manages to meet Henry on his way to Becket's shrine, and tells him the story of his wrongs so effectively that Henry recognizes him and is deeply moved. Later Lord Clifford meets Leicester, quarrels with him, and is slain. Queen Eleanor, accompanied by Cornwall, enters Rosamond's apartment and, according to a predetermined plan, so terrifies her by feigned anger and threats of violence that she pleads for her life and is led away to a convent. Under guard Leicester reveals himself to the prince as a villain and false friend, and advises him to seek his father's forgiveness. Rosamond is informed by Salisbury that Leicester has murdered her father, and that a merciful queen commands her to remain a prisoner in the convent. Cornwall and the queen tell Henry of their treatment of Rosamond. The prince obtains forgiveness, but dies as a result of poison he has taken. The king asks Eleanor's forgiveness, hears the news of Lord Clifford's murder, and seals up all in a bit of moralizing.

Genest thinks that Hawkins derived the character of Rosamond from Lyttelton's *History of the Life of King Henry the Second;*[19] but it is not likely that he got anything from the meager general account in that labor of twenty years, because it was not published until eighteen years after the appearance of Hawkins's play. One needs but to read Addison's *Rosamond* to see that Hawkins's plan to preserve the three main characters from tragedy is derived from that opera. To carry out this design, however, he transforms the furiously jealous, vengeful, and murderous queen of tradition into a gentle, forgiving wife who tells Cornwall, when they are planning to abduct Rosamond:

> The Person of my Rival shall be sacred:
> 'Twill pain me to dissemble Cruelty;
> For I have all the Softness of my Sex,
> But no Resentment, jealous Rage, and Malice,
> That wont t'inflame the Breast of injur'd Woman. (III, ii)

In preparing his audience for this departure from Eleanor's usual role, Hawkins avoids the mistake committed by his predecessor, who made her actions a surprise. On the other hand, the queen's threats, Rosamond's pleading for her life, the king's fear that murder has been committed, Rosamond's abduction to a convent, and the reconciliation of the royal pair—all these are in Addison; but there are certain variations in detail. Hawkins does not use the threat of either the dagger or the sleeping potion. He moves the scene from Woodstock to Canterbury, makes no mention of a labyrinth or bower, and Rosamond's

[19] For Lytteltons brief account, see the third ed., 6 vols. (London, 1769), III, 43-6.

woman, Harriana, has become merely a characterless creature introduced to make conversation at the opening of the third scene of the first act. Rosamond's second lover, too, is neither the trusted keeper nor the comic Sir Trusty of Addison, but a new character, the villainous Leicester.[20] Her aged father, Lord Clifford, appears here for the first time in any poetic version of the story,[21] and his use of disguise to bring to King Henry the sad story of his misfortunes is likewise a new invention. It is evident, therefore, that Hawkins used Addison's version of the story, but it should be pointed out that his departures from it, which are at times significant, and his omissions of certain traditional features of the story may have been inspired by eighteenth-century skepticism of the fabulous element in medieval history—an attitude which Hawkins no doubt shared.

That Mr. Addison's opera, as it was often called, still had its admirers is apparent from its republication in slightly altered form in 1767 as *Rosamond; an Opera, Altered from Mr. Addison's; the Music Entirely New Set by M.Arnold.*[22] The composer was Samuel Arnold (1740-1802). The only noteworthy alterations in the libretto were the omission of II, viii; III, i (which revealed Henry in a dream, a scene originally inserted to compliment the Marlborough family); III, ii; and the reduction of the original three acts to two.

Some vestige of the unusual twist which Addison and Hawkins had given to the legend of Rosamond may be detected in Thomas Hull's *Henry the Second; or, The Fall of Rosamond: a Tragedy,*[23] but it is not carried far enough to avert tragedy from Henry's Rose. After Hull had produced at Birmingham in the summer of 1761 an alteration of Hawkins's play,[24] William Shenstone, who was present at that performance, "signified his Wonder that such an affecting and *popular Tale* should not have found its Way to the Stage," gave him encouragement, and "suggested the character of the *Abbot;* in Order, as he said, to add a little more Business to a Story, which otherwise might be too barren to furnish Matter for five Acts."[25] But after Shenstone's death, February 11, 1763, Hull put aside his plan and did not resume

[20] For Leicester's only appearance in earlier versions, see *Look about You* (above, pp. 23-4), where he declares that the king's imprisonment of Eleanor is an act of justice for her murder of Rosamond.

[21] He had, however, been a stock figure in the early chapbook version for more than a century. See above, pp. 40ff., *passim.*

[22] London, 1767.

[23] The title continues: "as it was performed at the Theatre-Royal, Covent-Garden." London, 1774. It was produced May 1, 1773. The MS of the play is in the Larpent Collection at the Huntington Library. See *Catalogue of the Larpent Plays,* comp. by Dougald MacMillan (San Marino, California, 1939), no. 352.

[24] See above, p. 75.

[25] Hull's Preface, pp. i-ii.

work upon it until the beginning of 1773.[26] The printed version consists of five acts in blank verse and has a Prologue "written and spoken by the Author," in which he expresses admiration for "the plaintive Rowe," and an Epilogue by George Coleman the Elder. The scene is "Oxford, and Places adjacent."

The play begins with Clifford lamenting his loss of Rosamond through her sin with Henry. He seeks no vengeance against the king, but plans to reclaim his daughter. Prince Henry, who complains that his father has shared with him his throne but not his authority, and has wronged the queen by living in lust with Rosamond, is advised by Leicester to go to France and win the people to him. The Abbot, who hates the king because of Becket's murder, and wishes by keeping the prince in England to destroy Henry by civil war, encourages the queen to oppose the plan. But the prince is sent to France with Verulam, and the Abbot, compelled to change his tactics, tells Eleanor he will take care of Rosamond. In reality, however, he secretly hopes to bring about Henry's divorce from Eleanor and to make Rosamond queen, who will then rule Henry, just as the Abbot will rule her. In a cloister, disguised as an abbot, Clifford meets Henry on his way to Becket's shrine, and his feigned tale of having seduced his best friend's daughter wounds Henry's conscience. Rosamond decides to give up Henry and go into retirement. The Abbot opposes this by reminding her that she may yet displace Eleanor and become queen, but she scorns such a wicked scheme. Thwarted again, the Abbot incites Eleanor's jealousy by reporting to her that Rosamond is bent on becoming queen. He advises her to send Rosamond to some "dim, secure Retreat," but the queen decides secretly upon murdering her. Meantime, Clifford arranges to meet Rosamond at midnight to convey her to a convent. But Eleanor is there before him, and by threat of dagger compels Rosamond to drink poison, in spite of her plea for mercy. The king enters and rages at Eleanor, but Rosamond, forgiving both her wrongers, asks Henry to forgive the queen, to whom she says:

> Howsoe'er I loved,
> However guilty I have seem'd to you,
> This very Night I had resolv'd to leave
> These fatal Walls, and, by my Father's Guidance,
> Devote my future Days to Penitence.

Clifford enters, and, as he looks upon his dying daughter, declares that he will soon follow her to the grave. Eleanor, who confesses that her rage has unsexed her, resolves to give the rest of her days to "the sad Cloister and repentant Prayer," and Henry concludes the play with a speech on the "dread Effects of lawless Love."

[26] The Dedication to the memory of Shenstone is dated "Westminster, January 19, 1774."

"In the general Execution of the Piece," Hull says,[27] "I have paid a particular Attention to the *old Ballad*" (i.e., Thomas Deloney's ballad, which he had found in Percy's collection), and, he adds, "I am not conscious of any further Helps, excepting having adopted the Idea (not the Matter) of an Interview between the *King* and *Clifford* in the Monastery from Mr. Hawkins." This statement is fair enough, but not the whole truth. Hull must have known that the character of the villainous Abbot, suggested to him by Shenstone, had come straight from Bancroft's *Henry the Second* (1693), and that he goes about his evil work in much the same manner employed by his forbear. The minor character Verulam was probably suggested also by Bancroft's play. From Hawkins, in addition to the interview of Henry and Clifford (who, incidentally, does not merely complain of his misfortunes, as in Hawkins, but attempts to do something to extricate his daughter from her unfortunate position), which he admits to having borrowed, Hull took the idea of the intrigue of Leicester and the prince—though Leicester is no longer the murderer—and his villainy, since one villain was probably deemed sufficient, is transferred to the Abbot. From the same author, too, no doubt he derived the idea of having Rosamond make plans to retire to a convent—a plan carried out in Addison and Hawkins, but circumvented by Queen Eleanor in Hull.[28]

The year 1799 saw the publication of *Henry the Second, an Historical Drama Supposed to Be Written by the Author of Vortigern*,[29] i.e., William Henry Ireland, the Shakespeare-forger. The production of *Vortigern and Rowena* by Sheridan at Drury Lane Theater on April 2, 1796, as a play found among some newly-discovered manuscripts of Shakespeare, served to intensify the skepticism in certain quarters as to the authenticity of the documents, and so spurred the efforts of the attackers of Ireland that they eventually brought from him a confession of forgery. Neither of these plays had been included among the "Shakespeare documents" printed by Ireland's father in March, 1795, and *Henry the Second* was never produced on the stage.[30]

The play has twenty characters and a number of brief, repetitious, or even superfluous scenes, and its shows even less regard for the unities of time and place and for chronology and the common facts of history than the normal Elizabethan play which Ireland was attempting to counterfeit. In two earlier plays, those of Bancroft and Hull, much

[27] Preface, p. iii.

[28] In Deloney's ballad, Rosamond pleads with the queen to be allowed to retire to a cloister, but it is not likely that Hull would have developed the idea from Deloney while he had Addison's opera and Hawkins's play in mind.

[29] London, 1799.

[30] For a brief account of the controversy over the forgeries, see Sir Sidney Lee's article on "Samuel Ireland" in DNB. See also *The Confessions of William-Henry Ireland*, new ed., with an introduction by Richard Grant White, New York, 1874.

had been made of the villainy practised against King Henry and Rosamond by ecclesiastical partisans of Thomas À. Becket, but in Ireland's play, Becket himself is actually introduced upon the stage. This feature of the play, together with the political difficulties among the king, the queen, and their sons, rather overshadows the love affair between Henry and Rosamond.

The drama opens with Henry in France receiving word that he is to succeed Stephen as king of England. The scene then shifts to London, where Becket receives news from Theobald, Archbishop of Canterbury, that he has been appointed archdeacon of the church, and that the new king has already invaded Wales. At Clifford's castle in Wales, Henry comes upon Rosamond, falls immediately in love with her, and accepts her father's hospitality for the night. Before the coronation of Henry and Eleanor at Westminster, Becket is made chancellor, and later, in a soliloquy (p. 24), he boasts of his power, his personal use of the king's money, and his defiance of royal authority. At Woodstock Bower, Henry seeks to quiet Rosamond's fear of the queen. At Theobald's dying request Becket is appointed his successor. The queen, jealous and resentful of Henry's inattention to her, and thirsting for revenge, wins Becket's pledge to further her scheme to incite rebellion against the king, and, in return, promises to help him on his way to the papacy. Mowbray informs the king of Becket's treachery, and Becket seeks to withdraw his promise to Eleanor; but she holds him to his word. News comes that the King of Scotland has joined Eleanor and the princes in war against Henry. At Clarendon, Becket refuses to sign the king's act to try churchmen, resigns the chancellorship, and, after quarreling with Henry, informs Leicester of what as the king's confessor he has learned about Rosamond's bower:

Beck. Nigh Woodstock palace stands a secret bower,
The which, with so much art and skill is form'd,
That it defies the cunning of man's search!
For tho' you'd seem to pace it o'er and o'er,
You still return unto the self same spot,
By which you enter'd; known is the secret
Only to Mowbray and her Father, Lord de Clifford.

Lei. I shall with speed, relate this to the Queen.
And much will she applaud thee for this news. (p. 56)

Henry's knights, Morvele, Berison, Tracy, and Bryto, hear his expressed wish to be rid of Becket, and they promptly murder him. Eleanor, having already acted on the information which Leicester had brought from Becket, confesses to Prince Richard that she has poisoned Rosamond and made Lord de Clifford her prisoner. Eleanor, Richard, John, young Henry, and others are charged with treason. After Henry wins the battle against the Scots and the forces of Eleanor and the princes, he orders the Earl of Leicester and Hugh, Earl of Chester, to be executed, and the King of Scotland to be held for ransom; he pardons the princes, and, after hearing of Eleanor's murder of Rosamond, orders the guards to

> Bear her from my sight, lead her to prison,
> There let her pass the remnant of her days,
> In penitence and pray'r.—Bear her hence, I say. (p. 77)

The play ends with the king's declaration that he will go to Woodstock, there to

> take one last farewel,
> Ere that my Rosamond be laid in earth;
> Then cross the seas for France, where, as I hear,
> They fain again wou'd seize on Normandy,
> And curb our lion's glory.

Ireland was sufficiently ingenious as a forger not to depend for his ideas upon any sources with which his eighteenth-century audience or readers might be familiar. In fact, he so alters whatever he could have taken either from the tradition or from vague historical accounts, that I find it will-nigh impossible to point to any unmistakable sources for his play. His assignment of the meeting of Henry and Rosamond to Lord de Clifford's castle in Wales, whose hospitality he accepted, is unquestionably prompted by his reading of the old chapbook-version of the story. Leicester is neither the villainous lover of Rosamond, as in Hawkins, nor the powerful intriguer in league with the queen, as in Hull, but very little more than a carrier of messages from Becket to the queen, though he loses his head for sharing in her schemes. Rosamond's nurse has an insignificant role, as in Hawkins, but she reflects some borrowed light in her one scene, when, in the manner of Juliet's Nurse, she charges Henry with having a wicked look, and leads Rosamond away from him. We are told that Mowbray has the clue to the Bower, and he does appear to be Henry's confidant, but the play gives him no opportunity to serve as keeper and protector of Rosamond —his part in the earlier versions. Clifford, who had a fairly important part in the plays of Hawkins and Hull, is made a victim of Eleanor's vengeance because he was Rosamond's father and Henry's friend. The most striking departures from earlier treatments of the story, however, are the large part assigned to Becket and the relegation of Rosamond's poisoning to offstage action. Becket seems to have assumed in an indirect manner the villainous character of his partisans in Bancroft and Hull, in consenting to help Eleanor in her plans to get vengeance by murdering Rosamond and inciting rebellion against the king. But probably the most unexpected of Ireland's vagaries, from a dramatic point of view, is his avoidance of violence on the stage by having the murder of Becket and the poisoning of Rosamond—the most spectacular and dramatic of his episodes—merely reported to his audience. This is, to say the least, a rather naïve procedure for a man to adopt in forging a Shakespearean play.

Ireland's *Henry the Second* was written and published in the closing years of the eighteenth century—a period which had not produced a number of plays dealing with the Rosamond theme. But the work of Bancroft, Addison, Hawkins, Hull, and Ireland, spaced as it is through the century, is evidence of a continuing interest. It demonstrated to what extent and in what ways the story could be developed for dramatic performance. It set the pattern for a variety of types in the next century—tragedy, comedy, opera, burlesque, and pantomime—and indicated how the story of Rosamond might be combined with the struggle between Church and State as represented by those two great adversaries, Henry the Second and Thomas À Becket.

The continuing popularity of the Rosamond story on the English stage during the nineteenth century cannot be adequately measured by the number of plays which appeared in print, for some were performed, but were not published. *The Fall of Fair Rosamond*, for example, was given at the Surrey Theatre in Blackfriars Road on March 13, 1821, and *The Fall of Fair Rosamond; or, Woodstock Bower* was produced at the Royal Princess Theatre December 26, 1832.[31] W. H. Payne, the great pantomimist, who first appeared in London in 1825, became a "veritable master of pure pantomime. . . . Especially delightful, it is recorded [was], his love-sick Henry II in *Fair Rosamund*."[32] Pantomimes were acted at Covent Garden in 1838-40 and at the City of London Theatre in 1860-61.[33] George Lupino, of the famous Lupino ballet-dancers, in 1861 "had a solo dance in *Fair Rosamond* at the City of London Theatre, executing thirty-two consecutive pirouettes, finishing up with a 'double'."[34] An anonymous *Fair Rosamond* was presented at Astley's Amphitheatre, London, in June, 1860; F. C. Burnand produced for the usual Christmas harlequinade a pantomime, *Fayre Rosamonde; or, Harlequin Henry the Second, the Monarch, the Mazed Maid, and the Made Maize of the Arch Man*, at Greenwich, December 26, 1868;[35] and a burlesque tragedy, titled *Fayre Rosamond; or, ye Dagger and ye Poisoned Bowl*, by T. Cother, was performed at

[31] Allardyce Nicoll, *A History of Early Nineteenth Century Drama, 1800-1850*, 2 vols. (Cambridge, 1930), II, 448.

[32] See A. E. Wilson, *King Panto* (New York [1935]), p. 126.

[33] William D. Adams, *A Dictionary of the Drama*, London, 1904.

[34] Wilson, p. 242.

[35] Probably an adaptation of his earlier burlesque drama of 1862. See below, pp. 94ff.

the Theatre Royal, in Gloucester, April 19, 1869.[36] A four-act historical drama, W. M. Akhurst's *Fair Rosamond; or, The Days of the Plantagenets,* was produced at Sanger's Amphitheatre, March 3, 1873.[37] According to Erroll Sherson, "in 1878, a great spectacle," which, as its title suggests, may have been drawn from Akhurst's play, "was produced called 'Fair Rosamond: or the Day of the Plantagenets,' which was advertised as follows:

> SANGERS' GRAND NATIONAL AMPHITHEATRE
> (LATE ASTLEY'S)
>
> The proprietors do publicly challenge the entire profession to equal the exciting and effective scenes of the Battle of Bridgenorth!!"[38]

Adams records an undated performance of a "Christmas piece" by Robert Soutar on Fair Rosamond at Marylebone Theatre, London, with Josephine Neville as the heroine and T. A. Carr as Henry II; and a four-act play titled *Fair Rosamond,* by Brandon Ellis, was produced at Widnes Alexandra, August 7, 1893.[39] In addition to these plays, of which I can find no record of publication, one other, which though published, has been inaccessible to me, may contain some treatment of the Rosamond theme—C. E. Wallis's *The Life and Death of King Henry II; a Historical Drama,* published in two volumes at London in 1902-03.[40]

In some of the plays which revolve about the characters of Henry II and Thomas À Becket, Fair Rosamond does not actually appear, although in others some reference is made to her. She is, for example, referred to in the Prologue (p. x) of Henry James Pye's *Adelaide:*

[36] Reginald Clarence [i. e., H. J. Eldridge], *The Stage Cyclopaedia: A Bibliography of Plays* (London, 1909), p. 140. See also Adams, p. 480.

[37] *Stage Cyclopaedia,* p. 140.

[38] *London's Lost Theatres of the Nineteenth Century* (London [1925]), pp. 75-6.

[39] *Stage Cyclopaedia,* p. 140.

[40] Several plays and poems, whose titles may lead the reader to suspect that they deal with the theme of Rosamond and Henry, are in reality concerned with the tragic story of Rosamunda of the Lombards—a story with which the legend of Fair Rosamond was sometimes confused in the very early stages of its development. (See above, p. 8; 18, note 9.) I give here a partial list of the later versions of this story: *Rosamond: A Tragedy . . . translated from the German [of C. F. Weisse] by Fanny Holcroft* in *The Theatrical Recorder* (1805-06), vol. II, no. 12, pp. 359-97; *Rosamond; An Historical Tragedy* (London, 1829); *Rosamond. A Poem in Five Books,* no. 1 in a Series of "Melebaeus" (London, 1851); "Rosamond, Queen of the Lombards," in *Once-a-Week,* V (1861), 630-31; *Rosamond, a Poem* (London, 1864); H. B. Braildon, *Rosamond, a Tragic Drama* (London, 1875); A. C. Swinburne, *Rosamond, Queen of the Lombards* (London, 1899); John Pollock, *Rosamund,* a play produced at the Kingsway Theatre, London, in 1911; George Sterling, *Rosamund: A Dramatic Poem* (London, 1920); Gladys Brace Vilsack (Gladys Brace, *pseud.*), *Rosamond and Simonetta: Two Poetic Plays* (London, 1925).

A Tragedy in Five Acts (London, 1800); and in his *Woodstock*,[41] performed at Covent Garden Theatre, May 20, 1826, Isaac Pocock makes only such references to her (cf. p. 14) as were suggested by Scott's novel, on which the play was based. Sir Arthur Helps's *King Henry the Second. An Historical Drama* (London, 1843) and Laurence Binyon's *The Young King* (London, 1935) make no mention of her.[42]

As for plays on Thomas À Becket, in his *Becket: An Historical Tragedy* (London, 1832) Richard Cattermole, makes Queen Eleanor derisively point out Geoffrey, Earl [*sic*] of Lincoln, as "Rosamond's boy!" On the other hand, Douglas Jerrold's *Thomas A. Becket. An Historical Drama, in Five Acts* (1829),[43] Aubrey Thomas De Vere's *St. Thomas of Canterbury, A Dramatic Poem* (London, 1876), Alfred Waites's *Thomas Becket; or, The Mitre and the Crown* (Worcester, Mass., 1883), and T. S. Eliot's *Murder in the Cathedral* (New York [1935]) make no allusion to Rosamond. Alexander Hamilton, however, in his *Thomas A' Becket: A Tragedy in Five Acts* (1863), introduces some extravagances into the story when he represents Fitzurse as the illegitimate son of Henry and Rosamond, and has the dying Becket confess that he had been Rosamond's youthful lover until King Henry "won her from the truth, and steeped her in dishonor." Strangely enough, upon learning the truth of his origin, Fitzurse kills himself.[44]

But now I return to plays in which the Rosamond theme is fully developed. On February 12, 1813, a two-act drama, *Fair Rosamond*, was licensed by John Larpent. The manuscript of the play, now in the Larpent Collection at the Huntington Library, bears the endorsement "J. Faucit Theatre Royal Norwich–1813" and is dated by Larpent "Norwich, Feb. 12, 1813."[45] This is apparently the play performed in revised form at the Royal West London Theatre, October 18, 1821, and later printed as *Fair Rosamond; or, The Bower of Woodstock. A Grand Historical Drama, in Three Acts, by John Faucit Saville* [for John Saville Faucit].[46] The similarity of the titles suggests that this may have been revived later as the anonymous play, produced, according to Nicoll, at the Royal Princess Theatre, December 26, 1832.[47] It is a "grand" play, as the title suggests, if one considers the sixteen char-

[41] In *Dick's Standard Plays*, XX.

[42] For the latter author's brief but charming play on Fair Rosamond see below, pp. 118-19.

[43] In *Dick's Standard Plays*, no. 619, vol. V.

[44] New York [1863], pp. 104-05. The idea of Becket as a lover of Rosamond may have been derived from Mrs. Maberly's *The Lady and the Priest* (1851). For a discussion of this novel, see above, pp. 56ff. For other plays on Becket in which Rosamond has a part, see especially George Darley and Alfred Tennyson, below.

[45] See *Catalogue of the Larpent Plays*, comp. by Dougald MacMillan (San Marino, California, 1939), no. 1759.

[46] In *Dick's Standard Plays*, no. 788, vol. VII.

[47] See above, p. 82.

acters together with all the pages, citizens, officers, keepers, messengers, knights, and attendants who are called for in the cast, though there is nothing "historical" in it except the names of King Henry, Queen Eleanor, and Rosamond.

As the play opens, builders are erecting a triumphal arch in a London street to celebrate King Henry's victory over the rebels. Nero, the queen's fool, is babbling that she is plotting Rosamond's death. The queen commissions her conspirators to meet her at the Woodstock Bower on the following night. Nero places a note of warning by the king's bed, but it goes unnoticed. In the night, however, Henry dreams of Eleanor's threatening Rosamond with a dagger, starts up in alarm, discovers the Fool's note, confirms its contents from the Fool's lips, and, finding the queen missing and the palace attendants drugged, he and his knights ride to Woodstock "to save a damning crime." Meanwhile, at Woodstock, Sir Thomas Clifford, Rosamond's uncle and keeper of the bower, discusses with Alethea, the governess, the condition of their fair charge, who does nothing but read pious books, pray, grieve over her sins, and contemplate flight to a cloister. Thinking to comfort Rosamond, Sir Thomas relaxes his rule of admitting no one to the bower by welcoming a "Friar," who says he has a message from Rosamond's dead father, and a "Pilgrim"—actually Ruthenguen, a conspirator—and Queen Eleanor in disguise. After Sir Thomas withdraws, Ruthenguen, with a dagger at Rosamond's throat, forces her to drink poison. Her terrible death-agonies cause the queen to repent and to ask for Rosamond's forgiveness, which is granted. King Henry rushes in, and Rosamond, rousing herself to meet him, falls dead at his feet. After mutual recriminations, Henry and Eleanor separate, he to reform and she to "seal [her] penance by a life of solitude." The king indulges in some moralizing and commands that Rosamond be properly buried, and that a monument be erected to her memory.

Faucit has rejected almost all historical background, as well as the complicated political situation of Henry's reign, as motivation for his action. He has ignored also the usual love-scenes between Henry and Rosamond, and begins the action just before her death. All his characters are new except those of Henry, Rosamond, Eleanor, Sir Thomas Clifford, and Alethea. The last two are derived from the old chapbook, *The Life and Death of Fair Rosamond (c.* 1640),[48] although Faucit's play begins too late to reveal Alethea in her old role as procuress (in fact, she resembles rather the nurse or governess or maid developed in the eighteenth-century plays as companion or guardian of Rosamond), and for the same reason, Sir Thomas Clifford's part in first bringing Rosamond to Henry's court is omitted. Faucit actually departs from his

[48] See above, pp. 40ff.

source, however, in electing to trick Sir Thomas instead of overpowering him to gain admittance to the bower. The dream which warned Henry of Rosamond's danger was very probably suggested to Faucit by John Bancroft's *Henry the Second* (1693), because it appears in no other version; likewise, the disguised friar's pretending to come with a message from Rosamond's dead father bears a strong resemblance to Bancroft's device of having Rosamond's confessor trick Sir Thomas by pretending to bring a message and a gift from the King.[49] The disguise adopted by the queen and Ruthenguen is, however, a new invention. Rosamond's constant yearning for the life of the cloister, and Eleanor's vow, taken after witnessing Rosamond's death-agonies, to live a life of penance in solitude, are very probably inspired by Thomas Hull's *Henry the Second* (1774).[50]

A new development in the dramatization of the story is to be observed in the emergence of the one-act or one-scene play. Apparently, this particular form of the drama was born of necessity in the popular playhouses of London in the last century, where the more pretentious and more serious poetic dramas being performed at the few "legitimate" theaters would have been neither appreciated nor supported. In the rise of this form to popularity the story of Rosamond had some small part to play. The one-scene pieces in blank verse published by Mary Russell Mitford in 1827, however, can be considered only as forerunners of this development, composed, as they probably were, only for reading. But they suggest that a shorter piece in dramatic form had proved its attraction for the dramatist. One of eleven of these brief *Dramatic Scenes,* as she calls them, is *Fair Rosamond. A Tragedy,* "chiefly taken," she says, "from an old popular ballad of the same name in Bishop Percy's Reliques of Ancient English Poetry." "Some anarchronisms," she continues, "will, I fear, be found, besides those contained in the beautiful legend which forms the groundwork of my story; but at an age so remote, and with a subject, to say the least of it, apocryphal, a strict adherence to the old tradition will hardly be demanded."[51] This is a fair statement of what she has done.

The entire action takes place in an apartment in Rosamond's Bower at Woodstock. Rosamond is reminded by Mabel, her companion, that Pierce, the old forester, has urged her to retire to her secret bower, because he "dreads a quick surprise from powerful foes." At this warning she only laughs, as she tells of her dream of good omen—that she was a lonely spirit "in a bright world made up of sun and flowers." She is expecting Henry at noon, and she longs for her children, Geoffrey and

[49] For Bancroft see above, p. 70.

[50] See above, p. 78

[51] *The Dramatic Works of Mary Russell Mitford,* 2 vols. (London, 1854), II, 333.

William, who have been separated from her to prevent Eleanor's seizing them. She recounts to Mabel the story of Henry's wooing, how she first saw him when he was hunting on her father's estate, how they often met by the lake, and how she never knew that he was the king until she had confessed her love. Her story is interrupted by a noise without, but instead of her lover, the queen enters. Rosamond is forced to drink poison. King Henry enters and, surprised at the presence of Eleanor, he only gradually comes to realize what has been done. He orders Eleanor to be put to death, but Rosamond's plea that the queen's life be spared is granted. The queen is led away to prison, and Rosamond, thinking of her father and her children, dies in Henry's arms.

The author has concentrated her action upon the last hour before noon, and all pertinent events leading up to the crisis are related by Rosamond to her companion. The emphasis is laid upon Rosamond's beauty of spirit and Eleanor's cruel and vengeful character. There is nothing in the little scene to reveal dependence upon specific sources other than Deloney's ballad, to which the author admits her debt. Rosamond's dream of "sun and flowers" differs from earlier phenomena of the kind[52] in her regarding it as a dream of good omen. Old Pierce, the forester, is a sort of unofficial keeper of the bower, who replaces faithful Sir Thomas of Deloney's ballad. Henry's disguise, maintained until Rosamond confessed her love, has no precedent, with the possible exception of Warner's version.[53] Two innovations in the version of Mitford must be noticed, however. Deloney's ballad is not clear regarding the circumstances of the lovers' meeting, in fact, makes no statement concerning it. Mitford supplies this deficiency by telling how Henry met Rosamond while hunting on her father's estate. The other new feature is her reference to the children of Henry and Rosamond, little Geoffrey and William:

> My pretty gentle Geoffrey, and that boy
> Elder and bolder, my stout William,—he
> Who at some six years old already draws
> His father's sword, already flashes forth
> His father's spirit—my brave knightly boy!

Although they do not appear as characters in the playlet, this is the first definite reference to them in a literary version of the story.[54] The children were soon to become a prominent feature of a number of plays and novels written later in the century.

[52] See above, pp. 33, 45, 71-2, 85.

[53] See above, p. 15.

[54] In the seventeenth-century chapbook, it is true, Rosamond mentions her unborn child in her plea to Queen Eleanor. See above, p. 41.

February 28, 1837, saw the performance at the Theatre Royal, Drury Lane, of John Barnett's grand opera *Fair Rosamond.*[55] "The overture, and the whole of the music," according to the title-page, were composed by Barnett, but we are not told who was responsible for the libretto. That its author had misgivings as to the plausibility of its plot is made clear in an unsigned foreword: "It will be seen, in the following Opera, that some poetical license has been taken in the construction of the plot, &c. which was considered necessary for its general effect as a Drama." Without admitting the defensible argument that much opera, as drama, borders upon burlesque, as one reads Barnett's opera or recalls Addison's, one wonders whether the extravaganzas based on the Rosamond story later in the century found their inspiration in these works.[56]

The action takes place in 1154-5, and is confined to the De Clifford Castle and vicinity, Westminster Abbey, and Rosamond's Bower, presumably at Woodstock. Rosamond and her companion, Blanche, welcome home from the wars her father, Walter, Lord de Clifford, and her betrothed, Sir Aubrey De Vere. With them comes King Henry II disguised as Edgar, a Troubadour, who immediately persuades Rosamond to elope with him. Lord de Clifford and De Vere follow in pursuit. The second act discovers Rosamond outside a woodman's hut, impatiently awaiting the return of Edgar. De Vere arrives to promise paternal forgiveness if she will but return home. Edgar, accompanied by Sir Thomas Vaughan, the king's favorite, enters and quarrels with De Vere. De Clifford and Herbert rush in, and are about to lead Edgar away when they are interrupted by the arrival of Queen Eleanor. The third act opens with the coronation-ceremony in Westminster Abbey, where Rosamond rejects the suit of one Raymond De Burgh, a French follower of the queen, and kneels before the king to plead that she be allowed to wed Edgar. When the king speaks, she recognizes his voice as that of Edgar and becomes so much agitated that Henry confesses his love publicly. Queen Eleanor swears vengeance. In the last act she dispatches her masked follower De Burgh with a false message to Henry at Rosamond's Bower, warning him of a conspiracy against the state. He takes leave of Rosamond at once, and De Burgh then unmasks and renews his suit to her, only to be again rejected. Queen Eleanor, coming forward, dismisses all the attendants and forces Rosamond at dagger's point to drink poison. Henry and his party enter too late, but Rosamond asks him to pardon Eleanor, and he himself suddenly becomes contrite and promises to reform.

[55] *The Songs, Duetts, Choruses, &c. in Fair Rosamond, a Grand Opera, in Four Acts* . . . London [1837].

[56] For a discussion of burlesque plays, see above, pp. 82ff., and below, pp. 93ff.

The sources of the few scraps of material used by the author are not difficult to identify. The wooing of Rosamond at Clifford Castle (though not the king's disguise[57]), the rival lover who has the father's favor, Sir Thomas as keeper of the bower, and ruse of the message to gain entrance to the bower are derived from the chapbook version.[58] The role of Sir Thomas Vaughan, the keeper, is not clear. He leaves to guard the bower, but, like Lear's fool, he never returns and nothing more is reported concerning him. A second rival lover in the person of Raymond de Burgh, who after his rejection by Rosamond aids the queen in her plot, is a new contribution to the story. Original also is the maintenance of the secret of his identity by Henry, who keeps it even from Rosamond herself until the coronation, when its revelation brings on tragic results.

With the appearance of George Darley's *Thomas À Becket* in 1840[59] the story of Rosamond is for a fourth time (the earlier instances being the plays of Bancroft, Hull, and Ireland) entangled in the struggle between Becket or his partisans and King Henry. It will be recalled that in Ireland's *Henry the Second* (1799) Becket is represented as the reluctant aid of Queen Eleanor in her plot against Henry and Rosamond. In Darley's play, on the other hand, though the struggle is bitter between the two great champions, in a letter to the queen Becket stoutly refuses to stoop to such treachery. Written in blank verse and prose, the play is somewhat lengthy, contains many characters, and is complicated by unnecessary scene-divisions and by shifting scenes, some of which repel by their grotesqueness and lack of taste, and others are tiresome because they are superfluous. The story of Rosamond, which, incidentally, is handled better than that of the struggle between Henry and Becket, may be outlined as follows:

Queen Eleanor, suspecting the king's infidelity and unable to bring any one of her maids to confess a liaison with him, decides to consult a conjurer. Meantime, amid the luxury of Becket's palace, in a quiet spot removed from the gay revelling in progress, Henry tells Rosamond, known as *La Belle Disconnue,* that their love must be kept secret, and that after the death of the queen, who is now old, she will share the throne with him. Becket warns the couple of Eleanor's arrival, and although Rosamond escapes detection, she drops a ring which Henry had given her. Eleanor finds the ring and, disguising herself, consults a conjurer to ascertain its ownership; but Dwerga the dwarf interrupts the conjuring and announces that the device on the ring indicates that

[57] Which was used earlier only in Warner (above, p. 15), and in Mitford, where Rosamond does not learn that her lover is the king until she has told him of her love (above, p. 87).

[58] See above, pp. 40ff., 45. But for the ruse see Bancroft, above, p. 70.

[59] *Thomas À Becket. A Dramatic Chronicle. In Five Acts.* London, 1840.

Henry's love is named Rosamond. Eleanor questions her maids concerning all possible Rosamonds until she lights upon the one who meets all requirements—Rosamond de Clifford—and she vows to get revenge. Fitz-Urse dispatches Fier-À-Bras to Clifford Castle to bring Rosamond to the labyrinth at Woodstock, and appoints him warder of the bower. Rosamond's father, Lord de Clifford, who in his last illness is being cared for at Woodstock, advises Rosamond to abandon her plan to seek safety from Eleanor's jealousy by fleeing to Godstow Nunnery, and to cling to the king for protection. Meanwhile the queen asks Clifford's physician to poison him, but she is informed that such an act is unnecessary, since disease has already done its work. John of Salisbury, introduced as Rosamond's tutor, is at her request offered a bishopric by the king, but he refuses it, because he is a friend of the banished Becket. Queen Eleanor, who has sought to get from Becket the secret to the labyrinth, receives from him a letter of flat refusal: "I can be an open antagonist to a king," he assures her, "but a secret one to no man; neither can petty intrigues of the royal bower concern the Primate of all England." Eleanor's son, Prince Richard, who, she learns, has managed to meet the "Fairy Queen" in his wanderings about Woodstock, and who suspects something of his mother's intentions, refuses to reveal the secret of the labyrinth; but the queen's dwarf, Dwerga, who had laid down a thread as he followed Prince Richard through the labyrinth, provides her with the means of entry. By following the clue Eleanor and Dwerga come upon Rosamond as she is thinking of returning to Godstow Nunnery. By his antics and threats Dwerga frightens Rosamond, and when Eleanor reminds her that she is defenseless because her warder Fier-À-Bras "has been grave-sick these three days," she realizes that her pleas are futile and she drinks the poison. The queen and Dwerga leave the body in the bower. Meantime, Becket has been murdered by Henry's knights, and as Eleanor kneels before his corpse in Canterbury Cathedral, "The shade of Rosamond rises at the head of the Bier" and curses her. The guards see only the statue of a martyress, but Eleanor, terrified and ghostly pale, promises proper burial for Rosamond, faints, and is borne away.

Despite his obvious shortcomings in dramatic construction, Darley demonstrates much originality in his imaginative recreation of a simple story. He accepts the traditional components of the legend, but there is no positive indication that he has either derived anything from a specific source, with the possible exception of Ireland's *Henry the Second* (1799), or been noticeably influenced by any one of his predecessors. Unlike many of them, he makes no suggestion of Henry's seduction of Rosamond, and even goes so far as to make her father advise her to maintain her relationship to the king as the best defense against

Eleanor's jealousy. To a greater degree than his predecessors Darley emphasizes the queen's painstaking efforts to discover who Henry's mistress actually is, and he greatly increases the difficulties which she encounters in her attempts to learn the secret of the labyrinth. All her questioning of her maids, her extraordinary procedure in learning the the meaning of the device on the ring, her attempt to have Lord de Clifford poisoned, her application to Becket for the secret of the labyrinth, the accidental discovery of that secret by Prince Richard, her unsuccessful effort to bribe him to reveal it, and Dwerga's discovery and preservation of it for her use—all these are new features in the story. The surmounting of so many difficulties serves to accent Eleanor's persistence and her determination to use every available means to gain her ends. Her unwarranted cruelty to other persons than Rosamond—a trait of character emphasized by later writers—is here definitely indicated for the first time in the drama. True, in Ireland's play she takes Clifford prisoner, presumably for no other reason than that he is Rosamond's father,[60] and in Thomas Miller's novel, *Fair Rosamond* (1839), she attempts to stab Rosamond's son, young William.[61] As a means of revealing her dark and cruel nature, Darley causes her to seek to poison Clifford. Fier-À-Bras is the conventional warder or keeper, but here a new method is employed to get him out of the way: he has been "grave-sick these three days." The tutor of Rosamond in the person of that eminent scholar, John of Salisbury, is a new character, and nothing like the ring-episode is to be found in earlier versions of the story. Darley is the first author, also, to introduce into the tradition the grotesque element, represented by the conjurer and Dwerga the dwarf, and the supernatural represented by Rosamond's shade, which speaks to the queen at the bier of the archbishop.

Becket himself is not at all the Becket of Ireland's play—the abettor of Eleanor in her schemes against Henry and Rosamond. It should be pointed out, however, that Eleanor's unsuccessful attempt to get the secret of the labyrinth from him could have been suggested by Ireland's play, in which Becket as Henry's confessor knows of the goings-on at the bower but not of the secret ways of the labyrinth, and tells what he knows to Leicester, the queen's agent. In Darley, he knows the secret of the bower but refuses to divulge it. Moreover, Darley's Becket, though coldly efficient and overly ambitious, is at the same time a lover of pomp and gay living, and he actually lends encouragement to Henry's affair with Rosamond by entertaining them at his palace, by warning them of Eleanor's approach, and by refusing to yield up the secret at a time when a meaner man might have volunteered it. His

[60] See above, p. 80.
[61] See above, p. 51.

winking at the illicit love affair may be compared to a similar attitude assumed by him in Thomas Miller's *Fair Rosamond*, published in the preceding year. What we may have in Miller as well as in Darley is a hint which later led to the representation of Becket as a friend and protector of Rosamond—a development which culminates in a successful portrayal of him in that role in Tennyson's *Becket*.

CHAPTER V

THE DRAMA: 1840-1938

THE CONTINUED popularity of such forms of the drama as farce, burlesque, extravaganza, and pantomime in the illegitimate theaters of London during the middle years of the last century is too well known to be recounted here. The story of Henry and Rosamond was not one of the historical themes passed over by humorists who were in search of innocent subjects for caricature. In fact, a tendency in the direction of caricature can be detected early in the eighteenth century,[1] but it was not until the burlesque became popular as a form of drama on the stage that the story was treated solely from the point of view of the caricaturist. The first work of the kind was *Fair Rosamund, according to the History of England; a Musical, Burlesque. Extravaganza, in One Act,*[2] written by Thomas Proclus Taylor, son of Thomas Taylor the Platonist, and performed at Sadler's Wells Theatre early in 1838. The play begins in the mansion of Mr. Henry King, described in the cast of characters as "a Ruler, having been a Stationer," with his footmen, Fawnwell, Trencher, and Bones, singing:

> Hail to fair Rossy, Oh!
> Hail to fair Rossy, Oh!
> Mr. King gives her kisses
> And cheats our old missus,
> And drives from our bosoms each thought of woe.

They are making arrangements for a ball to be given in honor of Fair Rosamond, "a black girl, fair yet faulty," whom King is entertaining during his temporary respite from domestic boredom and the harsh treatment given him by his wife Eleanor, who is now out of town. Rosamond's father, Clifford, an American Negro, who enters with "a violin under his arm, and a blacking bottle and brushes stuck in his apron," offers his services as an entertainer at the approaching affair. Actually he is in search of his long-lost "darter, dat orient pearl," who at the time is quietly resting in King's bower in the garden. When the time comes to receive the guests, Rosamond falls ill and cannot be present, and news comes to King that his son, young Harry, has tangled

[1] See above, p. 74, note 13, and pp. 82ff., 84ff.

[2] London [1838]. Printed in *Duncombe's Edition [of the British Theatre]*, vol. XXV. The Dedicatory Letter addressed to Fix Cooper, Esq., is signed and dated: "Rose Cottage, Lambeth, May 13th, 1838."

with the law, and that his wife Eleanor has suddenly returned to town. To avoid disclosure of his secret affair, he orders Clifford to guard Fair Rosamond in her bower, where he discovers that his charge is no other than the object of his long search. A burlesque fight between King and Clifford ensues. Meantime, Eleanor enters, discovers Rosamond, and, threatening her, gives her a pill and a pinch of snuff. Rosamond swoons. The police arrive, Rosamond is revived, all is forgiven, and they all join in song. The action and stage-directions of the piece provide for sufficient horseplay, and the lines are made all the more amusing by the use of comic songs, curious puns, a questionable American Negro dialect, and quotations from Shakespeare's tragedies rather cleverly introduced for their incongruous effects.

On April 21, 1862, Sir Francis Cowley Burnand, the well-known humorist, produced at the Royal Olympic Theatre, his *Fair Rosamond; or, The Maze, the Maid, and the Monarch,* "an entirely new, but historically true version of the ancient strange story."[3] It is a one-act play of five scenes in verse. The "characters" affixed to the various *dramatis personae* give a foretaste of the punning and the broad humor which run through the entire play. Henry, for example, is "a very *affable* monarch, but *not able* to keep himself out of mischief," while Sir Trusty, the "First Lord of the Pleasury, in the King's confidence," is "a character whom the author has managed to steal from Addison." The peasants are "a very harrowing sight, with nothing to say for themselves, but plenty to till," the Executioner is "devoted to his chop," and Rosamond, "like a celebrated character of the present day, is a *Blonde-in* a difficult situation."

As the play opens, a group of peasants are making merry with the jester Wynkyn before the gates of the royal hunting-lodge in Hereford. King Henry, accompanied by Sir Trusty, enters in search of Rosamond. Sir Pierre de Bonbon and Ralpho, sentenced to death for poaching, are saved by the sudden appearance of Rosamond, who pleads for them. Queen Eleanor enters in time to sense a rival. Rosamond leaves and Henry rides off in pursuit of her. Eleanor attempts to follow, but her horse carries her away in the wrong direction. The scene shifts to Hereford Academy, where Rosamond and the orphan, Margery, are in the keeping of an old virago of a schoolmistress named Grideline. Sir Pierre, in love with Rosamond, and Ralpho, in love with Margery, enter; discovering that Grideline is not at home, they attempt to elope with their sweethearts. But Grideline returns through a secret panel, and the girls are separated. The king and Sir Trusty, returning in disguise, ask Grideline for temporary shelter. The queen, much dishevelled by her wild ride, and the girls enter, and all retire to their respective rooms. Sir Pierre and Ralpho, returning with the intention of

[3] In Thomas Hailes Lacy's *Acting Edition of Plays* (London [1850ff.]), LV, 8-43.

carrying off the girls, suddenly come upon Queen Eleanor walking in her sleep in parody of Lady Macbeth. Sir Pierre hides in a well, and when King Henry and Sir Trusty rush in, such confusion ensues that the queen falls into the well with Sir Pierre, and the king and Trusty carry off Rosamond and Margery. The scene shifts to the entrance to Woodstock Bower, where Wynkyn is shown studying a message commanding him to have the bower in readiness for the king and "a friend." Margery, however, charms him into handing over the "guide-book" containing the secret of the labyrinth. The king enters, carrying Rosamond, who has fainted. Upon reviving, she spurns his advances, but he carries her off to the bower. The queen enters, disguised as a gypsy, tells Margery's fortune, and promises more revelations in exchange for the secret of the labyrinth. But Sir Trusty rushes in, the queen hides, and Margery, in repulsing Sir Trusty's attempts to get the "guide-book", throws in his face a ball of worsted yarn. She rushes off into the bower, unwinding the thread as she goes, and it provides a clue to the secret ways of the labyrinth. By means of the clue the queen, carrying her dagger and bowl, manages to reach Rosamond. As the latter is about to drink the poisonous draught she is saved by Sir Pierre, who has hacked his way in. Henry enters, promises Eleanor to reform, and gives the lovers his blessing. The three pairs of lovers are ready for marriage as the curtain falls.

From this synopsis, it is clear that the main object of Burnand's parody is Addison's opera *Rosamond* (1707). The author steals from it not only Sir Trusty, as he humorously confesses, but the name Grideline as well, and Henry's frantic search for Rosamond at the opening of the play probably points to a similar situation in Addison (I, vi). Moreover, the songs which Burnand employs serve to accentuate the association. The burlesque of the messages, the clue, the adventitious arrival of Sir Pierre to rescue Rosamond, and other travestied features of the story may have been directed at the unpublished plays and pantomimes which had appeared a few years earlier, and were still fresh in the memories of the theater-going public. It is probable, also, that his use of elopement, disguise, the sudden appearance of Queen Eleanor, and the French lover of Rosamond would recall to some members of the audience another opera, the *Fair Rosamond* of John Barnett, although it had been produced, to be sure, thirty-five years before.[4] I suspect, however, that Burnand was directing his shafts of ridicule more generally at some features of three novels—those of Miller, Egan, and Maberly—which had appeared from 1839 to 1851. Eleanor's disguise as a gypsy may be a glance at Faucit's play, where she and her follower enter disguised as pilgrim and friar.[5] One of the chief reversals of

[4] See above, pp. 88-9.
[5] See above, pp. 84-6.

tradition, and probably a ready cause of merriment for the audience, was the exhibition of royalty as victims of comic mischance—the spectacle of the queen's being carried off on a runaway horse, walking in her sleep, and falling into a well, and, similarly, Henry's loss of Fair Rosamond to the rival lover, who, according to tradition, had never met with anything but scorn from her.

The play must have met with sufficient success, for on December 26, 1868, Burnand produced at Greenwich a pantomime announced as *Fayre Rosamonde; or, Harlequin Henry the Second, the Monarch, the Mazed Maid and the Made Maize of the Arch Man,* which may well have been an adaptation of his play designed specifically for the Christmas harlequinade.[6]

From Burnand's play or pantomime, or from both, Frederick Langbridge probably took the hint for his one-act "anti-historical burletta" in verse, *Fair Rosamond's Bower; or, The Monarch, the Maiden, the Maze, and the Mixture,*[7] published with the motto *Dulce est desipere in loco,* apparently at a much later date than Burnand's play.[8] The brief piece has but three characters, Henry, Eleanor, and Rosamond, who are described in much the style used by Burnand, and the play displays the same fondness for strained punning; but songs and local references are more frequent than in the earlier play. The action may be sketched briefly. In scene one, Henry, while out hunting, meets Rosamond. Scene two shows Eleanor weeping alone in her boudoir, singing,

> Harry, dear Harry, come home to me now,
> Return to your spowsie so true, etc.

In scene three, Henry reveals to Rosamond his love and discloses his identity. As they are making plans for the wedding, Rosamond inquires whether, when she is old and ugly, Henry will love her still. His reply is a fair sample of the style of the play:

> *Henry*. Till ballet girls, obeying state decrees
> Have petticoats descending to their knees;
> Till modern ladies on their faces wear
> Roses that grow in Nature's own parterre,
> Till female suffrage grist brings to the *Mill,*
> And genuine cures are wrought by Cockle's pill,
> (For by this potent patent—so I'm told—
> The sick are not so often *healed* as *sold*),
> Till comic papers fail to make us weep,

[6] For a brief comment on the Christmas pantomime, see Allardyce Nicoll, *The History of Early Nineteenth Century Drama,* 2 vols. (Cambridge, 1930), I, 154.

[7] In Lacy's *Acting Edition of Plays,* LXXXIV, 3-18.

[8] The Lacy edition gives no date for the performance or publication of the play, but Langbridge's period of productive activity began about 1881.

Low Church divines to "Rock" their flocks to sleep.
Till critics read old Tupper's sonnets through,
And see the drift of Swinburne's ravings too,
Till London cabmen generously forbear
To charge their victims twice the proper fare,
Till milk becomes connected with the cow,
Maid of my heart, I'll love thee e'en as now.[9]

To Rosamond's astonishment, Henry blurts out an admission that he already has a wife "as hideous as sin,/ Addicted to low company and gin." Incidentally, Eleanor, against all plausibility, is made to enter twice in the scene, latterly to sing "Put it down to me" as the villain in the piece—no doubt as a parody of opera. In scene four, laid in the bower, the stage-direction reads in part: "Enter Eleanor, L., carrying under one arm a 'cup of cold p'ison,' a table-spoon, and a large bottle, labelled, 'Anderson's Bug Destroyer.' In the other hand she holds a dagger and a skein of wool, in accordance with the legend, which states that in this manner only could the mazes of the bower be threaded. An old cloak is thrown over her royal apparel, and she speaks in a tone of suppressed rage, and occasionally, bitter irony." Hearing Henry and Rosamond approaching, she hides. Henry, who must leave for France, pays a tearful farewell to his mistress, who falls on a couch and sleeps. Eleanor wakes her and reveals her identity, whereupon Rosamond cries for help. They then sing a duet to the air "Champagne Charlie" and toss for the bowl or dagger. Rosamond loses, drinks, and falls on a couch. Henry enters to drag Rosamond off the stage. He and Eleanor fight, but when Rosamond awakens and reenters, he is reconciled to his queen, and all three sing together.

In Langbridge's play the obvious intention is to burlesque not alone opera in general, but, especially in the denouement, Addison's *Rosamond* in particular. That the author may also have had in mind John Winspere's play, *Fair Rosamond* (1882), is suggested by Henry's meeting with Rosamond while he is hunting in the woods, by the use of the clue in threading the labyrinth, and by use of a sleeping potion instead of poison.[10] Henry's proposal of marriage to Rosamond, even though he is already wed to Eleanor, is perhaps an indication that Langbridge had in mind the second-marriage problem, not only as it was treated in Winspere's play, but as it had been ingeniously varied by writers of the preceding generation.

Plays of the kind we have just considered, as far as I can judge, contributed little or nothing to the literary tradition of the story, but the fact that popular writers such as Burnand and Langbridge should

[9] Pp. 8-9.
[10] See below, pp. 104ff.

have burlesqued the story of Fair Rosamond before London audiences is an indication that readers of the middle generation of the last century had become well acquainted with the legend through the increased number of novels and plays that had come during those years from the pens of Barnett, Miller, Darley, Egan, Maberly, Wightwick, Winspere, and Swinburne.

But it is now necessary to return to the serious drama. Nothing of the kind appeared from the publication of George Darley's *Becket* (1840) until 1851, when George Wightwick brought out his five-act, blank-verse tragedy of *Henry the Second,*[11] with a dedicatory letter to his good friend William Charles MacCready, the famous actor. It is a play which departs from the tradition in several marked respects. The story begins after Fair Rosamond has entered Godstow Nunnery, and although she has a considerable part in the action, she never once appears on the stage. Furthermore, Princess Alice, who, though a historical character, had never before been brought into literary versions concerned with either Henry or Rosamond, is so favored by the king that she is falsely suspected by the queen to have taken Rosamond's place as his mistress.[12] Finally, the untraditional character, Sir Walter Clifford, is presented as the son of Henry and Rosamond and lover of Princess Alice.

A great part of the play is concerned with the conflict between Henry and Becket, which ends with the latter's murder in spite of Henry's attempts to prevent it. Since this thread of the plot has no interdependent connection with the story of Henry and Rosamond, it may be put aside at once. Princess Alice, though betrothed to Prince Richard, does not love him, but is loved by Sir Walter Clifford, the son of Henry and Rosamond. She is represented as sympathetic to the king in his troubles, as one who can soothe and divert him because she reminds him of his lost Rosamond. Through her also Sir Walter has been able from time to time to see his mother at Godstow Nunnery. From Rosamond he bears a message to Henry expressing the hope that they may always remember each other without bitterness, but insisting that she must be thought of henceforth as dead. As Princess Alice plays the organ, the king becomes rapt in a reverie, "the subject of which is manifested by a phantom picture of Rosamond at prayers in her cell" (I, ii). Somewhat later Alice brings another message to Henry from Rosamond:

[11] London and Plymouth, 1851.

[12] A contemporary of Wightwick, in a well-known work first published in 1840, which may have been known to him, discusses the charge that King Henry seduced Princess Alice, the betrothed of Prince Richard. See Agnes Strickland, *Lives of the Queens of England*, 8 vols. (Philadelphia, 1893), I, 280, 283, 286. See also above, p. 3.

> Go tell the King I do not fear to say
> I love him *now;* since now I truly feel
> That Heaven is lov'd before him. Should *he* feel
> As I do, he may, then, with loyalty
> To Eleanor, preserve in innocent thought
> The memory of poor Rosamond. (II, ii)

Eleanor interrupts Alice and Henry to express her suspicion of their frequent conversations, which, she thinks, cause Alice to neglect Richard, and Henry to fail in his duty to his sons and the state. By suggesting to Richard that the king is making another Rosamond of Alice, the queen sows in his mind the seeds of malice against his father. After the murder of Becket, Queen Eleanor and Richard openly charge Henry and Alice with adultery. Richard thereupon releases her from her vow, and she and Sir Walter decide to proclaim their love. As the king grieves for the loss of his rebel sons, Henry, Geoffrey, and John, Alice brings news of the death of Rosamond. Perhaps as a foreshadowing of the epitaph she was to have on her tomb, Henry laments her passing:

> And, thou art gone, too lovely Rosamond!
> The "Rose of all the World," I rudely pluck'd,
> Lies low in death: but O, I'll not believe
> Corruption can possess it. Rather say,
> That its surviving fragrance scents the air
> Which fondly sighs above its faded form,
> And drinks its ling'ring sweetness.

The four assassins of Becket, now about to become monks, enter to ask Henry's blessing, which he grants as he includes himself as a fifth needing forgiveness for the foul deed. Richard, too, enters to ask forgiveness, and to report that Prince John is alive but in rebellion still. Henry forgives all, even John, joins the hands of Alice and Sir Walter, names Prince Richard his successor, and dies.

Apparently, the major problem which Wightwick set for himself was so to choose and arrange his characters and incidents as to intensify the tragedy that came to King Henry. He therefore discards the happy story of Henry's clandestine love and begins his plot after Fair Rosamond had placed herself by her retirement to Godstow Nunnery beyond the reach of her lover. The king's partial responsibility for the murder of Becket, the jealousy and scheming of his queen, the rebellion and loss of his sons, the death of Rosamond—all are made to press down upon him their heavy weight in the last hours of his life. And throughout the play one feels that the influence of absent Rosamond serves only to deepen the tragedy crowding upon a hapless and lonely man, as we see him seeking some small comfort in the company of Princess Alice and Sir Walter—the only remaining links to the one woman he loved—

whose love for each other seems to give to him promise of the enduring happiness he and his Rose had never fully realized.

In 1860, at the age of twenty-three, Algernon Charles Swinburne published his first significant work, *The Queen-Mother and Rosamond,* two poetical dramas in blank verse, "affectionately inscribed" to Dante Gabriel Rossetti. A first draft of the *Rosamond,* which had been completed before the end of the preceding year, though it won the approval of William Morris, had shortly thereafter been destroyed.[13] The strong Pre-Raphaelite influence upon the play appears in the poet's overfondness for elaborately-wrought passages of vivid and sharp sensuous detail. These create a sort of dream-world of love and jealousy and imminent death through which his characters slowly move without much reference to reality. The author reveals a lack of dramatic invention, a certain sporadic unconsciousness of action, so that the incidents by which the business of a play is ordinarily advanced are either sparingly alluded to or are not clearly defined because they are entangled or buried in phrase-making. Swinburne has isolated the love story from the historical events—war, politics, and the struggle between church and state—with which many of his predecessors since John Bancroft had interwoven it. In so doing, he has concentrated the scope and diminished the complexity of his play, which has but five scenes and is only about one-third as long as its full-length companion-piece, *The Queen-Mother.* He uses but five characters, and the action seems to run from spring (i, 13) to late summer (v, 1), and the scene shifts back and forth between Woodstock and Shene. In the dialogue between Rosamond and Constance, which makes up the first scene of the play, much care is taken to emphasize Rosamond's beauty, and to portray her as a forceful, sophisticated woman who suffers no remorse for her lost virtue, but, quite the contrary, derives satisfaction from her fame as the beauteous mistress of a loving king:

But I that am
Part of the perfect witness for the world
How good it is; I have chosen in God's eyes
To fill the lean account of under men,
The lank and hunger-bitten ugliness
Of half his people; I who make fair heads
Bow, saying, "though we be in no wise fair
We have touched all beauty with our eyes, we have
Some relish in the hand, and in the lips
Some breath of it," because they saw me once.

. . . .

I that have held a land between twin lips
And turned large England to a little kiss;
God thinks not of me as contemptible.[14]

[13] Harold Nicolson, *Swinburne* (New York, 1926), p. 55.

[14] *The Complete Works of Algernon Charles Swinburne,* ed. Sir Edmund Gosse and Thomas James Wise, 20 vols. (London, 1925-27), VII, 207-08.

Constance, her virtuous but self-righteous and censorious companion, who serves as a foil to Rosamond, a sort of sounding board for the proud one's ideas, fades from the play at the end of the first scene and is never heard of more. It is not clear whether she provides Bouchard with the secret of the bower.[15] At any rate, Sir Robert de Bouchard, who is in love with Queen Eleanor and feeds the fire of her jealousy, knows the way to Rosamond, and leads the queen thither. Confronting Rosamond, the queen offers her the choice of dagger or poison, and, as always, she chooses the latter. One wonders whether, in the weakness and resignation to her fate displayed by her in her last moments, she is consistent with the strong woman revealed to us in the first scene of the play. As Eleanor observes the effects of the poison on her victim, Henry, accompanied by Bouchard, enters, and after realizing what the queen has done, curses her:

> God,
> Curse her for me! I will not slay thee yet
> But damn thee some fine quiet way.[16]

As Rosamond dies in his arms, Henry, shutting out his surroundings, mutters frenzied speeches over her, somewhat in the manner of Romeo or Lear.

Swinburne gives the reader only brief glimpses of the antecedent action, makes no provision for a keeper of the bower, disregards the difficulty presented by the labyrinth, and, instead of the traditional governess who is either a procuress or a welcome companion, he creates the self-righteous and vindictive Constance. He is the first writer in the tradition to represent the queen's attendant as her lover who helps her to the bower. Bouchard's relationship to Rosamond is not made clear, however. The poet's use of the French songs sung by Rosamond in her bower is new, as is also the entire scene in which Bouchard and Eleanor in the ante-chapel at Shene plot Rosamond's death while the choir-boy extravagantly praises Rosamond's beauty and sings Latin verses in the outer passage. These novel devices, whose possibilities may have been suggested by the opera, are additional means of creating atmosphere—which seems to be the chief of Swinburne's artistic aims.

[15] Cf. end of scene i, where Constance says,

> Let the queen make some tale,
> A silk clue taken in the king's spur's gold,
> No fear lest I be taken; and what harm
> To catch her feet i' the dragnets of her sin
> That is so full of words, eats wicked bread,
> Shares portion with shame's large and common cups,
> Feeds at lewd tables, girds loose garments on?

[16] P. 254.

Of greater complexity in its action is Charles Grindrod's full-length drama, *King Henry II,* with which he won the Henry Spicer prize for historical drama in 1874, and which he published in 1883 together with his plays on Henry I, Henry III, Edward II, Edward V, and James I[17] —all except the *King Henry II* in four acts, and all in blank verse, with a sprinkling of prose for the low characters. The theme of the play is the struggle between Henry and Becket, but considerable space is given to Henry's love of Rosamond and the queen's plot against her. The paths of Becket and Rosamond never cross, although he is aware of Henry's love, and, when informed of the plot of the queen and the Monk of Godstow against Rosamond, he does what he can, as a hunted man, to have the Monk apprehended and sent to Henry for punishment. It is a well-constructed play save for its implausibility in the handling of time.

The drama opens with Henry's knights, Fitzurse, Tracy, Brito, and De Morville, swearing vengeance against Becket as a traitor. Becket announces to Henry that since the Pope has annulled all oaths taken at Clarendon, the archbishop must therefore renounce his own. Eleanor asks the king to banish her rival, but he attempts to divert the queen by reminding her of her own infidelity to King Louis, implying that what she has heard is only idle gossip. She is unconvinced, however, and resolves to discover his secret for herself. In the company of a Monk of Godstow, she lurks about Woodstock Park and tries in vain to learn the way to the bower. The king and his lords are entertained by dancers at Woodstock, and after dismissing his companions, Henry is joined by Rosamond, who sings a song and tells him of her fears, and particularly of a dream that has troubled her—a dream of "a cowled monk, with flaming eyes, and brows that should affright the darkness by their frowning!" (p. 82) As Henry leaves her, she attaches "a skein of silk" to his spur in order that he may follow the thread back to the bower upon his return. The Monk, who with Eleanor has been watching the while, plucks the clue from the king's spur as he passes through the labyrinth. For this he is rewarded by the queen and sent to the king's leech to procure poison. All this has been observed by the Prior of Godstow and is revealed to Becket, whom he encounters in flight from the knights of the king. Becket orders the Prior to apprehend the Monk and send him to Henry for punishment, and with the help of some fishermen he himself manages to escape to Normandy. As Henry again takes leave of Rosamond, he gives her a goblet, from which they drink to their love. Though still fearful and troubled by the memory of her dream of the monk, Rosamond, after Henry's departure, sleeps. Eleanor and the Monk steal in and drop poison into the cup. Rosamond awakes and, to allay her fever, drinks from the cup. She staggers toward

[17] *Plays from English History,* London, 1883.

the bed, cries for help, and falls dead. In Bayeux Palace, Henry, now reconciled with Becket, who is back in Canterbury, is sad. Clarence sings to him,

> Sad was the heart of Dido,
> When her lord would go—

a song which Rosamond had used to sing at Clifford Castle when she was

> a merry girl,
> With ringlets that did romp it with the wind
> Which strove to kiss her cheek. (p. 117)

A herald enters with the news that Becket has firmly resolved to renounce his oath, and the king explodes in anger against the prelate. The knights, who overhear this, excuse themselves, and Henry, reminded of their probable murderous intentions, orders pursuit of them. The Monk of Godstow, who is brought in to confess the murder of Rosamond, is ordered by the king to be executed, and the queen is to be confined to Godstow Abbey for life. At Canterbury Cathedral, meanwhile, after Becket is mortally wounded by the knights, Henry enters to repent of his rash outburst, to condemn the cruel deed of the knights, and to hear words of good advice from the lips of the dying archbishop.

Grindrod's treatment of the Rosamond story is noteworthy for its exclusion of certain traditional elements which usually appear in the more elaborate versions of the story. There is, for example, no rejected rival lover, no keeper of the bower, no maid or servants about Rosamond. Rosamond's father is not introduced, and there is no reference to Henry's meeting with Rosamond, beyond the hint that it took place at Clifford Castle, or to a marriage with her, or to children by her. There is no indication that Becket is acquainted with her, and her story is not so closely fused with the main plot as in, for example, Darley's *Thomas À Becket* or Tennyson's *Becket*. Like Darley, however, Grindrod makes much of Eleanor's difficulty in learning the secret of the labyrinth. The choice of a churchman—the Monk of Godstow—as the evil agent of the queen carries the mind back to the Abbot and Bertrard in Bancroft and to the Abbot in Hull,[18] except that Grindrod's Monk does not represent either Becket or his cause. Indeed, the more sympathetic and more faithful portrayal of Becket that characterizes nineteenth-century writers in general is clear in his and the Prior's opposition to the evil plot of the Monk. Rosamond's warning dream of the Monk is, of course, a variation of a device used first by Bancroft in 1693, and later by certain versions of the chapbook and by Pattison,

[18] See above, pp. 70-1, 78.

Faucit, and Ranking.[19] A possible influence of the opera is to be detected in the use of dancers before the king and his lords, and of songs sung by Rosamond and by Clarence, though the actual introduction of the songs could well have been suggested by Swinburne's play.

The most significant innovation in Grindrod, from an artistic point of view, is his original handling of the poisoning incident. A surprising number of later writers accept the folk-conception that Rosamond, when commanded to drink, offered little or no opposition beyond a plea to be spared. This somewhat naïve treatment of human nature is discarded, or perhaps evaded, by Grindrod when he has the Monk drop the poison in the goblet while his victim sleeps, and then shows Rosamond rising in the night and in her fevered and nervous condition quite plausibly drinking from the cup used but a few hours before in a love-toast. This plausible and tragically ironic episode is the best and most original thing in Grindrod's play.

Writing under the pseudonym of John Winspere, the Reverend Vincent John Leatherdale published in 1882 his *Fair Rosamond. A Comedy Drama. In Four Acts.*[20] The term "comedy drama" is perhaps somewhat misleading, because even though the three main characters survive, the action involves many threats of violence and three violent deaths, two of them on the stage. The play, which is in blank verse, covers a period of five years (1150-55) and is perhaps unduly complicated by a number of minor characters and incidents, as if the author were resolved to make every scene interesting in itself without giving sufficient attention to the unified effect of the whole play. For the sake of clarity I shall neglect some of these minor incidents in my synopsis.

While hunting in a glen in the vicinity of Clifford Castle, Henry meets and falls in love with Fair Rosamond, in a scene reminiscent of the meeting of Ferdinand and Miranda. He obtains her father's consent for a future marriage. A "clown" by the name of Robin Roughhead, who has long been a distant lover of Rosamond, serves as her attendant at the Castle. Roger, Earl of Hereford, who has accompanied Henry to the Clifford home, is also smitten. Rosamond's father is killed in battle, and Hubert de St. Clare, Constable of Colchester and loyal friend of King Henry, becomes her guardian. After an interval of three years, a priest comes to Woodstock Castle, where Rosamond and her maid, Editha, are now guarded by Hubert, and tells Rosamond that Henry has already married Eleanor of Aquitaine. His attempt to make love to her is repulsed by a drawn dagger. Henry, who is adamant to Hubert's suggestion that Rosamond should be sent to a convent, swears

[19] See above, pp. 32, 35, 45, 70-1, 85.

[20] London and New York, n. d. I find no evidence that the play was ever performed.

he will "marry her by priest and book." Upon Henry's promise that once he is wedded to Rosamond he will divorce the present queen, Hubert agrees, and a secret marriage is provided for and later effected. Two years later the queen, who has become very jealous at reports which she has received of goings-on between Rosamond and Henry, enlists the services of Hereford to "ferret out what secret lies i' the woods" about the bower at Woodstock. After following Henry through the maze twice before, only to become lost in the woods, she one night attaches a thread of green silk to a bush, so that by unwinding it as she follows him through the labyrinth she will be able to mark the way in and out. By this means she is enabled to discover Rosamond's secret bower. For her next visit she asks Robin Roughhead, who, strangely enough, is now serving as her apothecary, to prepare a deadly poison for her, but Robin outwits her by substituting a harmless drug. She and Robin surprise Rosamond in the bower, and when Rosamond learns for the first time that Eleanor's marriage to Henry actually antedates her own by six months, she rushes at the queen with drawn dagger. She is arrested in the act by two pages, who refuse to stab her at Eleanor's command. Eleanor herself hesitates to use the dagger, and Robin steps forth with his cup of "poison." Rosamond drinks and falls to the floor, and the queen, after weakening in her impulse to kill Rosamond's baby in its cradle, leaves Robin alone with the "body." After Rosamond is revived, Robin conveys her, Editha, and the babe to Godstow Nunnery. Robin and Editha plan to be married. Hereford, who seeks by a trick to take Rosamond from the nunnery, is killed by Hubert, and Hubert himself, after communicating to Henry at the siege of Mortimer the news that Rosamond has taken the veil and so is beyond his reach, steps in the path of an arrow intended for his king, and dies.

For the groundwork of his story Winspere made use of the more recent of the chapbook versions already discussed, *The History of Fair Rosamond, the Beautiful Mistress of King Henry the Second.*[21] Henry's meeting with Rosamond while he was hunting on the Clifford estate, the birth of a son, the reconciliation after long separation, the delay of the marriage, the introduction of a priest, the failure of Eleanor's plans for Rosamond's death, and the latter's retirement to Godstow Nunnery—all these are to be found in the chapbook. But upon these Winspere has made some significant variations: they fall in love at the first meeting, not after many meetings, as in the chapbook; the marriage actually takes place in Winspere, whereas in the chapbook the marriage is long deferred and never takes place; the priest is a would-be lover, not a blabbing confessor and pander; and Eleanor is prevented from killing Rosamond, not by the paralyzing effect of her

[21] See above, pp. 46-8.

victim's beauty and meekness, but by the good offices of Rosamond's friend and former attendant, Robin Roughhead. Instead of assigning to Rosamond a keeper, who as a result of her rejection of his love proves treacherous and discloses the secret of the labyrinth to Eleanor, Winspere provides Hubert de St. Clare, the loyal friend of King Henry and faithful guardian of Rosamond's bower.

Other features of Winspere's play may be accounted for by his acquaintance with the novels of Thomas Miller (1839) and Pierce Egan (1844).[22] From the former he probably derived the idea of antedating Henry's marriage to Eleanor of Aquitaine by his secret union to Rosamond, as well as Robin's substitution of a harmless drug for the poison, though in Winspere the act is motivated, whereas in Miller it comes as a surprise. The character of Robin Roughhead bears some slight resemblance to that of Miller's Oliphant Ugglethred. But Winspere owes an even greater debt to Egan's novel. From him he may have taken the cue for complicating his plot by increasing the rival lovers from the traditional one to three, as well as the incident in which the queen displays her cruel nature by threatening to kill Rosamond's babe in its cradle. From Egan, too, he certainly derived both the names and the characters of Editha, Rosamond's maid, and Hubert de St. Clare, the loyal friend of Henry and guardian of Rosamond. At the end of the play he disposes of these characters precisely as Egan had done. Editha promises to marry Robin, just as in the earlier work she was to marry Aldred, Rosamond's faithful attendant; and Hubert de St. Clare, like Hubert de St. Clair, met his death by interposing his body between an arrow and his king. Another feature of Winspere's play which may have been suggested to him by Egan's novel is the greatly strengthened character of Rosamond. She is no longer the meek beauty of tradition (though her charms smite king, earl, priest, and clown) who is passive in misfortune and awed by the commanding presence of a queen. She is wise in her replies to Henry's wooing, is quick to defend herself against the advances of the priest, and, when she is threatened by the queen, rushes at her as one whose only impulse is to strike her enemy first.

In view of the fact that the alteration of the story to avert tragedy for the heroine began with Addison and reached full circle in Winspere, it may be significant at this point to review the development of the problem which various authors set for themselves. In Addison's opera, it will be recalled, the queen had herself administered a harmless potion, so that while Rosamond was unconscious she was to be taken to a convent. Hawkins altogether abandons the idea of the potion, and causes Eleanor's anger and feigned threats of violence so to terrify her victim that she is led away to a convent. Thomas Miller makes

[22] For a discussion of these novels, see above, pp. 50-6.

Oliphant Ugglethred, the agent of Eleanor, prepare, unknown to her, an innocuous draught, and Rosamond of her own volition enters Godstow Nunnery. In Egan's novel, Aldred arrives just in time to slay the Saracen slave and to make Eleanor prisoner, and Rosamond, after recovering from her fright, retires to Godstow. In the nineteenth-century chapbook the meekness and great beauty of Rosamond cause the queen to drop her weapon, and Rosamond promises to see Henry no more and enters Godstow Nunnery. Maberly has Becket, in revenge for his rejection by Rosamond, excommunicate and persecute her, so that, driven temporarily insane, unwelcome at her own home, and bereft of all help, she dies at Clairvaux Convent. The good queen Eleanor—the only good one, incidentally, in the entire tradition—of Smith's version forgives Rosamond and persuades her to enter a nunnery. Wightwick avoids the problem altogether by beginning his action after Rosamond has already retired to Godstow. Finally, Winspere, taking his cue from Miller, solves the problem by having Rosamond's former attendant, Robin Roughhead, betray Eleanor by substituting a harmless drug for the poison which the queen had hoped to administer, and by taking her, after she had revived, to Godstow Nunnery. No two of these solutions of the problem are alike, though they all plainly aim at the same thing—to save Rosamond from Eleanor's poison, and to see her finally removed to the safety of a convent. If any explanation for this persistent tendency be required, it might be said that the rise and continuation of this development were probably inspired by the desire of more modern authors to bring the story into line with historical fact without sacrificing too much of one of the most attractive features of the old legend.

In December, 1876, Tennyson began work on his tragedy of *Becket*, and although first proofs of it had been printed by 1879, it was not actually published until December, 1884.[23] On July 20, 1886, an adaptation of the play, arranged by Edward William Godwin in three acts with a pastoral prologue, was performed in Canizzaro Wood, at Wimbledon, with Lady Archibald Campbell as Rosamond, Bassett Roe as Henry II, F. H. Macklin as Becket, Maud Millet as Margery, and Genevieve Ward as Queen Eleanor.[24] Tennyson himself witnessed

[23] See *Alfred Lord Tennyson: A Memoir by His Son*, 2 vols. (New York, 1911), II, 193.

[24] W. D. Adams, *Dictionary of the Drama* (London, 1904), p. 131. The adaptation was printed with the following title: "Pastoral play of Fair Rosamund. Adapted and arranged in three acts, for the open-air, by the late E. W. Godwin, from Becket, for Lady Archibald Campbell, by special permission of Alfred Lord Tennyson, poet laureate." [Albany, New York, 1895.] I have used the Yale University Library copy.

Godwin has used as the scene of the play the "Outskirts of Rosamund's Bower," has added songs and a garlanded procession of countrymen led by a small orchestra, and has reduced the *dramatis personae* of the original play approximately by half.

the performance and thought the scenes "very effective among the glades of oak and fern."[25] Sir Henry Irving, who had refused the play in 1879, asked leave in 1891 to produce it, "holding that the taste of the theatre-going public had changed in the interval, and that it was now likely to be a success on the stage."[26] It was accordingly arranged for representation, and had its first performance on February 6, 1893, at the Lyceum Theatre, London, with Sir Henry Irving in the title role, W. Terriss as Henry II, Ellen Terry as Rosamond, Genevieve Ward as Queen Eleanor, and Kate Phillips as Margery. It had more than fifty performances, and in September, 1893, it was performed at San Francisco, and in 1904 in the English provinces, with Sir Henry Irving in his original role.[27]

As a drama of the struggle between Becket and Henry, between the church and the crown, the play is beyond the scope of this study. What had several times been attempted before, the interweaving of the Rosamond legend with the story of that struggle, had never been crowned with the artistic success that Tennyson achieves. Most of Tennyson's predecessors who dealt with the difficulties of Henry and Becket appear to be so intent upon the great issue in which their protagonists are involved that they seem deaf to the appeal of human interest which the story of Rosamond presents, or if they do give prominence to it, they sometimes fail to achieve an artistic fusion of the very diverse plots. In Tennyson's *Becket,* however, Rosamond has a sufficiently prominent part in every act, and she is brought into such close relationship with all the other main characters as to produce a unified, well-balanced literary work.

Tennyson's interest in Rosamond was not a recent one, for in 1833 he had introduced her into his *Dream of Fair Women,* where, echoing Daniel's Rosamond, she expresses regret that she had not been "some maiden coarse and poor," and is haunted day and night by the "dragon eyes of anger'd Eleanor" (11. 253-6); and before 1842 he had written a little song called "Rosamond's Bower" in which he gives her thoughts and fears as she sits alone listening for noises in the night outside.[28] But his early acquaintance with the story was apparently inadequate for his play, since when he set to work on *Becket,* we are told, he made

The difficulties between Henry and Becket are almost ignored, and the action, limited to the relations of Henry, Rosamund, and Eleanor, is ended by Henry's outburst in the first scene of the last act of the original play: "Will no man free me from this pestilent priest?" and the stage direction, "Knights *draw their swords,* with the cry of 'Kings men, Kings men.' "

[25] *Memoir,* II, 326.

[26] *Ibid.,* II, 196.

[27] Adams, pp. 131-2.

[28] The poem is quoted in *Memoir,* II, 197. Cf. a poem by Scott, above, p. 34.

use of materials furnished him by Bishop Lightfoot.[29] There is, however, no information as to the nature or amount of help the bishop gave the poet. There is reason to believe that it consisted of little more than the stock features of the traditional legend together with some ideas which he had collected from Miller's novel and Darley's play, and that Tennyson altered and added to these at will from his reading and experience to satisfy the requirements of an original artistic design which he imposed upon the story.

As it weaves itself through the historical struggle between King Henry and Archbishop Becket, which, incidentally, was the major theme in Tennyson's mind, the story of Rosamond is so recreated and enriched by the fertile imagination of the poet, and its integrity is so well preserved that it can perhaps be very readily examined in comparative isolation from the historical elements of the play. An account of the love affair is introduced into the Prologue of the play. Already secretly married to Rosamond, Henry, while playing chess with Becket in a castle in Normandy, tells him that he fears "the Queen would have her life," and shows him a chart of the concealed bower he has built for her in England:

> See, first, a circling wood,
> A hundred pathways running everyway,
> And then a brook, a bridge; and after that
> This labyrinthine brickwork maze in maze,
> And then another wood, and in the midst
> A garden and my Rosamund.[30]

Rosamond is at the moment residing in a bower in Anjou, and Henry exacts a promise from Becket to look after her after her return to her "English nest." Eleanor, who has heard just enough of the conversation to become suspicious, persuades Sir Reginald Fitzurse, who, like De Tracy and De Brito, once loved Rosamond, and, like them, has been rejected, to help her get her rival out of the way. In the first scene of the play (back in London), Rosamond flees from Fitzurse to Becket's house for protection. He gives her an armed escort to her bower. Eleanor's retainers fight with Becket's because Fitzurse has reported that Becket had been caught with "a wanton in [his] lodging." Unable to get the chart from Becket, Eleanor vows to stir up trouble for the king. The second act opens in the bower with Rosamond vainly pleading Becket's cause with Henry. Little Geoffrey, their son, is introduced. After giving Rosamond a little cross which Eleanor had given him, and telling her he must follow Becket to France, Henry

[29] See *Memoir,* II, 193: "Bishop Lightfoot found out about Rosamond for me."
[30] *Works,* ed. W. J. Rolfe (Boston and New York [1898]), Prologue, 11. 84ff.

bids her farewell. In act three, Rosamond tells Henry of her loneliness and apprehension, of how her keeper, John of Salisbury, has taken to drink, and how her best maid has died and has been replaced by one Margery, whom she dislikes and fears. In the wood outside Rosamond's Bower, Eleanor and Fitzurse prowl about, reconnoitering the vicinity to discover the entrance to the labyrinth. Becket hears of this and returns to England to protect his charge. Little Geoffrey, who has followed "a bit of yellow silk here and there," hoping to find his way to the fairies, comes out of the maze and meets Eleanor. Thinking that she is the good fairy, he leads her back into the bower, which is unguarded because John of Salisbury has had a stroke. Eleanor and Geoffrey come upon Rosamond, and, Geoffrey being dismissed, Eleanor demands that her rival shall drink the poison or be stabbed to death. Rosamond pleads for her child, offers to bury herself in oblivion, and when Fitzurse enters and demands her for himself, refuses to drink. Infuriated at the sight of the cross given Rosamond by Henry, Eleanor raises the dagger to strike, but Becket rushes up from behind and catches hold of her arm. Eleanor pretends to him that she was only trying to frighten her, but he refuses to believe her. He tells Rosamond that she must go to Godstow Nunnery:

> Daughter, the world hath trick'd thee. Leave it, daughter;
> Come thou with me to Godstow Nunnery,
> And live what may be left thee of a life
> Saved as by a miracle alone with Him
> Who gave it. (IV, ii, 209-14)

Eleanor goes to France to madden Henry against Becket, and, after displaying the cross which she had taken from his mistress, tells him that Becket had taken Rosamond to Godstow. Henry angrily mutters, "Will no man free me from this pestilent priest?" and Eleanor's retainers, who overhear his outburst, leave at once for England and Canterbury to accommodate him. Meantime, Rosamond, who has heard that Becket intends to excommunicate the king, goes in the disguise of a monk to Canterbury Cathedral with the hope of obtaining his promise to abandon his plan. But the knights enter and kill Becket, and the play ends with Rosamond kneeling in prayer over his dead body.

Probably one of the most significant features of Tennyson's *Becket* is his portrayal of Becket as the protector of Fair Rosamond, and of her as his admiring friend and Henry's mistress, as she assumes the attractive role of peacemaker between the two great champions of Church and State. At the very beginning of the story Becket is informed by Henry of the illicit affair and made protector of Rosamond by royal command. As her guardian, he is given a chart which provides him with the secret to the hundred pathways of the labyrinth which must be threaded in order to reach her in her retreat at Woodstock. It is to him that she flees for protection from Fitzurse and his band; it is Becket himself who arrives at the bower in time to prevent her death at the hand of Queen Eleanor; and it is he who places his charge in Godstow Nunnery, where she will be beyond the reach of her enemies. He had given his word to the king, apparently out of consideration and concern for the unfortunate victim of Henry's lust, and with his customary thoroughness he carries out his promise to the letter. It is superb tragic irony that for his act of safeguarding the king's mistress from her enemies, Becket should have been repaid with death by a band of knights who thought they were acting at the kings behest, and that Rosamond, in the magnificent and reverential scene with which the play closes, should go in disguise to the cathedral just before the tragedy to plead with Becket not to excommunicate her royal lover, and should remain to kneel in prayer over her friend's dead body.[31]

There can be no question that Tennyson, or Bishop Lightfoot, obtained suggestions for these, as well as other untraditional ideas, from Thomas Miller's three-volume historical romance, *Fair Rosamond: or The Days of King Henry II* (1839).[32] That work contains the only instances—though Darley's play of the following year affords a few slight parallels—in which Becket plays the role of protector of Rosamond, and she that of peacemaker between him and the king. In Miller's novel Becket advises the king to hide her in Normandy—a piece of advice not acted upon, though the idea probably suggested to Tennyson his creation of a bower in Anjou for her, similar to the one in England. On several occasions Becket seeks to allay the queen's suspicion of the love affair, and it is upon his advice that Rosamond is placed in the labyrinth at Woodstock. Again thinking to protect her from her enemies, Becket, when banished by the king, asks her to accompany him to France. Moreover, Miller's original invention of casting her in the role of pacifier is the only instance of the kind earlier than Tennyson. On the other hand, Tennyson has disregarded in his source the abductions and sieges, the role of Clifford, and the affair of the minstrel, Pierre Vidal, and Rosamond's maid, Maud. More important, however, is the result of his discarding Oliphant Ugglethred's substituted potion to save Rosamond from death, in favor of having Becket as her protector arrive in time—a common device since Ban-

[31] Contrast this denouement with the final scene of Maberly's novel, *The Lady and the Priest* (1851), in which Rosamond's rejected lover, Ranulph de Broc, leads the same band of knights to the slaying of Becket, for the wrongs the priest had heaped upon her. See above, p. 58.

[32] See above, pp. 50-3.

croft first used it—to stay the hand of the queen. This solution of the problem of sparing Rosamond is new in the tradition.[33] It strengthened Becket's role as protector and led to the strange and tragically ironic situation of his being martyred as a service to the crown for his act of preserving the king's sweetheart from death.

Tennyson derived some ideas from George Darley's *Thomas À Becket* (1840), in which Becket encourages the affair by entertaining the pair of lovers in his palace, by warning them of the queen's approach, and by sternly refusing to yield up to her the secret of the labyrinth. But Darley does not reveal a sufficiently close relationship between Becket and Rosamond to suggest the parts which Tennyson has assigned to them. Nevertheless, that Tennyson was acquainted directly, or indirectly through Bishop Lightfoot, with Darley's play is clear on at least three counts. John of Salisbury is given a role in the Rosamond story in no earlier version except Darley's, in which he serves as her tutor, and out of loyalty to the banished Becket, refuses from the king a bishopric tendered him at her request. The keeper of the bower, however, is one Fier-À-Bras, who, according to Eleanor's statement, cannot come to the assistance of Rosamond because he has been "grave-sick these three days." Now, Tennyson curiously fuses the two roles. He assigns to John of Salisbury the traditional role of keeper of the bower and makes his addiction to drink result in a stroke that incapacitates him in the crisis. Moreover, for Tennyson's scene in which little Geoffrey, thinking Eleanor the queen of fairies, innocently leads her through the labyrinth to his mother in her bower, I can find no hint of a source in earlier versions except the scene in Darley's play in which Eleanor unsuccessfully questions her son, Prince Richard, who in his wanderings about the labyrinth had learned the secret way and had seen the "Fairy Queen." The results of the act in the two instances are unlike, but in both, Eleanor seeks the clue from a child who has had some sort of experience with the queen of fairies. Finally, in view of these affinities of the two poets, it seems very probable that Becket's stout refusal, in Darley's play, to reveal the secret to the queen created in Tennyson's mind the idea of his refusal to give her the chart to the labyrinth.

Tennyson's handling of certain traditional features of the story deserves some attention, because in almost every instance he has so varied them as to make them contribute to the artistic design and effect of his play. By the time Tennyson began to write his play, the children of Henry and Rosamond—a nineteenth-century addition to the story—had already come to be a regular feature of the tradition,

[33] Although it bears some resemblance to Aldred's prevention of Rosamond's death in Egan's novel (see above, pp. 53-5). For a review of the variations played upon this type of denouement, see above, pp. 106-07.

but the role which Tennyson assigns to little Geoffrey, as he innocently leads Queen Eleanor to the bower of his mother, is designed to give the effect of tragic irony. Moreover, instead of making Rosamond's maid either the procuress or the colorless companion of tradition, Tennyson may have taken a hint from Swinburne's Constance, when he created the suspicious and vindictive Margery (a name that could have been derived from Burnand's play),[34] who serves to emphasize Rosamond's unhappiness, and to intensify the atmosphere of apprehension and suspicion that surrounds her. Moreover, not content with the single rejected lover of the older tradition, or with the two employed by his immediate predecessors, Tennyson must have three—all among the knights who were to slay Becket. Here, the dramatist has undoubtedly risked the danger of implausibility to achieve the irony of tragedy. Fitzurse, the leader of the band, who in revenge for his rejection by Rosamond can persecute her, and, still as Eleanor's agent, actually renew his suit while Eleanor stands by and threatens death to her—this villain can be matched only by one other rival lover in the tradition, one Raymond de Burgh of Barnett's opera,[35] whom Fitzurse so much resembles that one is led to believe that Tennyson had seen or read that work. Finally, as he had planned his denouement, he could not, without risking an anticlimax, give any account of Henry's detection of the queen's part in the plot against Rosamond, nor any hint of the punishment meted out to her for her treachery. The omission of this traditional feature of the story can be understood by any one who reads with imagination and sympathy the final scene of the play.

In the same year in which *Becket* was published, two ladies, Katherine Harris Bradley and her niece, Edith Emma Cooper, under the masculine pseudonym of Michael Field, published a two-act tragic drama, *Fair Rosamond,*[36] a caricature of the legend, which presents as the heroine a unique Rosamond who

> Was no rich, crimson beauty of old line,
> As fabled in proud histories and lays;
> No Clifford, as 'tis boasted; but, in fine
> A girl o' the country, delicately made
> Of blushes and simplicity and pure
> Free ardour, of her sweetness unafraid;
> For *Rosa Mundi,* of this truth be sure,
> Was nature's Rose, not man's; as ye shall see
> In this sad tale of lover's destiny.

In other words, the authors seem to say, here you will see what would

[34] See above, pp. 94ff.
[35] See above, pp. 88ff.
[36] *Callirrhoë: Fair Rosamond.* New York, 1884. I have used the limited edition published by the Ballantyne Press, London, 1897.

have happened to such a poor country maid as the traditional fallen Rosamond often wished she might have been. If they have a serious intention in the theme of the play, they are evidently bent on demonstrating that if Rosamond had been the poor country girl whom they portray, the misfortunes of her and her family would have been even worse than those which were visited upon that noble lady, Rosamond de Clifford. Certainly, the outcome of the hypothetical experiment, viewed in terms of fatalities, is more swiftly devastating than was ever before incorporated into the story of Rosamond and her circle.

The play opens at Woodstock, where architect Mavis reports to King Henry that the labyrinth, shaped like a rose, will be completed within five days—"even to the silken clue." The king privately tells Sir Topaz of his love for Rosamond, the country maid, and appoints him "Warden of the labyrinth and guardian of the lady." Sir Wilfred de Lacy, betrothed to Beatrix, pretending to purchase a hunting-dog from old Michael, the foster-father of Rosamond and Margery, but actually spying upon the king and his sweetheart, comes upon the girls as they are talking of the fairies, and is immediately fascinated by Margery. Back at court in Winchester, Sir Wilfred informs the queen that in the wood he had seen Henry kiss Rosamond. She is furious at the news, and later quarrels with Henry. Now that the labyrinth is completed, the king goes to Woodstock, finds Rosamond asleep under a beech tree, and after much persuasion induces her to spend the night with him in the bower. Meanwhile, in another part of the wood, Sir Wilfred comes upon Margery as she watches the fairies dance, and persuades her to go away with him. The next morning Margery appears in the finery given her by Sir Wilfred, and as Rosamond is trying to dissuade her from further reckless conduct with him, he appears and threatens to tell the queen of what goes on at Woodstock if Margery is not allowed to elope with him. They leave Rosamond to think on her weakness of the preceding night, and Sir Topaz conducts her back to the bower. At Winchester the king resolves to leave for France to put down a rebellion, and Queen Eleanor and Sir Wilfred immediately plot to murder Rosamond. When Margery returns to tell old Michael the truth about her experiences with Sir Wilfred, he dies of shock. Rosamond, still grief-stricken over her father's death, is tenderly bidden farewell by Henry, while the queen, professing to be Rosamond's and Margery's long-lost mother, accompanied by Sir Wilfred, procures poison from Ellen Greene, the old witch, and persuades Margery to lead them to Rosamond in the bower. As Rosamond, awaiting the king's return visit, combs her hair in the moonlight, Queen Eleanor enters and offers her a choice of poison or a dagger. Rosamond at once stabs herself, and the queen leaves. Margery enters, and seeing what has happened, stabs Sir

Wilfred, and drinks the poison. Henry enters and grieves over Rosamond. He curses Sir Wilfred, pities Margery, and announces his intention of erecting for Rosamond a stately shrine "at Goddeshill . . . 'mid the sisterhood of blessed nuns."

Although known circumstances of date of composition do not favor the inference that borrowing is involved, certain resemblances between this play and the Rosamond story in Tennyson's *Becket* seem to be something more than the result of coincidence. The introduction of the witch, Ellen Greene, the name Margery, her interest in fairies, and her unwittingly leading the queen to her sister's bower have a correspondence to Tennyson's allusion to witches (III, ii), to the name of Rosamond's maid, and to his use of Geoffrey's interest in fairies to lead Eleanor to his mother's bower. These coincidences, and I offer them as nothing more, may be the result of a common source which I have not come upon in my reading. The bower itself, the keeper (under a new name, of course), and Sir Wilfred, serving as Eleanor's agent, are all traditional. Even old Michael, the foster-father of Rosamond, as he dies of grief, brings to mind a similar fate which befell Lord de Clifford in some earlier versions. On the other hand, there are some new things. As has been pointed out, Rosamond is a radically different character from the Rosamond of tradition, and she is seduced after the completion of the labyrinth. The parallel seduction, involving Rosamond's sister and Eleanor's hireling, is without precedent, as is also the witch, Ellen Greene, as the purveyor of the queen's poison. In no other version in the tradition does Rosamond ever attempt suicide by dagger. The authors are by no means novel, however, in displaying their greatest originality in the means devised for gaining entrance to the bower—Eleanor's posing as Margery's long-lost mother. It is curious, but perhaps reasonable, that King Henry should never suspect Eleanor's part in the plot, but to assign unqualified naïvete to such a man is as radical a departure as the transformation of Fair Rosamond to an innocent country girl of easy virtue. In fact, one is compelled by charity to believe that the gallimaufry tumbled together by the authors was intended as nothing more than a travesty of the grotesque and other extravagant features to be found in certain versions of the preceding generation.

In June, 1890, Barrett Wendell published in *Scribners' Magazine* a brief dramatic sketch of one scene called *Rosamond.* In reprinting it in his *Raleigh in Guiana, Rosamond and a Christmas Masque* in 1902, he refers to the circumstances of its composition: "Some years ago, a friend of mine—then a young girl—asked me to make her a version of the story of Rosamond. In so doing, I only turned to the old ballad, as it stands in the old editions of Percy's *Reliques,* and swiftly translated the narrative into versified dialogue, with whatever alterations and additions chanced to occur to me."[37] As a type of dramatic composition the piece closely resembles the "dramatic scene" inaugurated by Mary Russell Mitford in 1827.[38] Since both authors reveal that they have used the same source—Deloney's ballad as found in Percy—a comparison of the two versions immediately suggests itself. Both limit the scene to the bower at Woodstock, narrow the action to the encounter of Queen Eleanor and Fair Rosamond, and write in blank verse. Wendell differs, however, in practicing the perhaps too severe economy of dispensing with the maid, whom Mitford's more fertile dramatic invention employed to create a feeling of expectancy and apprehension by means of her conversation with her mistress. A further difference is that in Wendell's version Rosamond does not die on the stage, and King Henry does not appear. At the opening of the play Rosamond is represented as reading a letter from Henry. The queen enters, but is not at first recognized. She discloses her identity, tells Rosamond that Sir Richard, the keeper (for Sir Thomas in Deloney), who attempted to bar her way, has been killed. In her plea that her life may be spared, Rosamond emphasizes the reciprocal love between herself and the king, but finally admits that she has done great wrong both to herself and to Eleanor, receives the vial of poison, and, at Eleanor's command, retires to her chamber to drink it. Wendell's paring away of any preparation for the action, his failure to create feeling in the characters or to arouse in the audience any sympathy for them, and the weakened denouement render his brief play rather ineffectual.

Another play similar to Mitford's in scope and conception is the one-act blank-verse tragedy, *The Labyrinth,* by Oliver W. F. Lodge, which was performed by the Pilgrim Players on October 14, 1911, and printed in the same year.[39] The plan of the play bears a closer resemblance to that of Mitford than the version which we have just considered. The conversation between Rosamond and Yolanda, her maid, with which the scene opens, serves to create a feeling of anxiety because the king has not arrived at the appointed time, to give a sense of the pervading fear of the queen, and to reveal Rosamond's mood. Her heart is heavy as she ponders the fate of true love. In an aside she says:

> Am I some *Minotaur* that must be hid
> Or else the King is shamed? Nay, rather she
> Who shares his bed and hates him, the French Queen,
> Tis she is monstrous. They who love give all
> As I have given, and tis Love's alone
> To give so.

[37] New York, 1902, p. 7.
[38] See above, pp. 86-7.
[39] Pilgrim Players Series, no. 2. London, 1911.

She asks Yolanda to sing a song, and then dismisses her maids. They go out, and Rosamond kneels and prays that her lover may soon come. Queen Eleanor enters "with a clue wound to a ball," makes herself known, and depicts herself as a victim of the king's infidelity. When Rosamond says, "Madam, from the depth/Of my sad heart I pity you," Eleanor hurls at her the epithet "harlot," and says she came not for pity. Rosamond defends herself against the charge, but when the queen presents her the poisoned drink, resolves not to fight, because her fate, she feels, is sealed, as has been that of every tragic heroine of history who has greatly loved. After she drinks the poison, Henry enters, but she dies without a word. Soon realizing what has happened, he swears vengeance against the queen:

> *Q. El.* I am thy lawful wife,
> False King, and this thy harlot. God shall judge
> Between us, and not thou.
>
> *The King.* Aye, God shall judge.
> But first will I, and thou shalt swift be sent
> To abide God's judgment. Thou dost very well
> Shake and look pale. I see thee howling soon.
> But she will flower in Heaven as in the world,
> Unchanged, immortal, in the bowers of God.
> Curtain falls.

The plan of the scene, it is clear, is essentially the same as that of Mitford's play, from which Lodge may have taken a suggestion, though the characters in his play are much more forcefully represented, and many of his speeches possess greater poetic merit. The use of songs by Yolanda to cheer Rosamond reminds one of a similar device in the plays of Swinburne and Grindrod. Rosamond's feeling, however, that as the victim of an overmastering love she is caught in the relentless web of fate, is a new feature of the story.

Maurice Baring published in 1912 a collection of *Diminutive Dramas* which had earlier appeared separately in *The Morning Post.* Among these brief scenes in prose, most of them based on historical or legendary characters and episodes, and all of them written from a twentieth-century point of view, is one entitled *Rosamund and Eleanor.*[40] The scene is "A room in Rosamund's house, 'The Labyrinth,' Woodstock," and the characters are Rosamond, her maid Margery, and Queen Eleanor. Apparently taking his idea for the scene from Sir Francis Cowley Burnand's burlesque, *Fair Rosamond* (1862),[41] Baring introduces Queen Eleanor in the disguise of a shabbily-dressed gypsy

[40] No. xix, in *Diminutive Dramas* (Boston and New York, 1912), pp. 189-97.
[41] See above, pp. 94-6.

fortune-teller who is made welcome by Rosamond's eagerness to have her fortune told, though we are not informed of the means used by the queen to thread the labyrinth.[42] The dialogue proceeds much like that of the modern lady and gypsy woman, until Eleanor's "revelations" touch upon the king's infidelity, and draw from Rosamond an unfavorable character-sketch of her rival. Suddenly swelling in anger and unable longer to maintain her disguise, Eleanor discloses her identity, displays to Rosamond a dagger and a vial of "painless poison," and gives her two minutes to choose between them. When the appointed time has elapsed, Rosamond throws both dagger and poison to the floor, calls her maids and keepers—Margery, Rosalie, Topaz, Anselm, Richard, Thomas[43]—and has them turn the queen out of doors.

As in the other diminutive dramas of the collection, Baring has stripped the Rosamond story of all mystery and romantic glamor, and presented characters who act as modern men and women, according to his views of human nature, would act in such a situation. This kind of treatment does not permit Rosamond to wilt and cringe into submission and to drink the poison at the command of her rival. She has at last become the twentieth-century woman who does the very practical thing of treating her royal rival as an equal in a contest for the same stakes, and accordingly she deals with her as one woman to another.

A unique extension of the legend is conceived and executed with charm and skill by Laurence Binyon in his *Godstow Nunnery,* a single-scene play performed in Mr. Masefield's theatre on Boar's Hill in 1929, and published in September of the following year.[44] As the central figure in the scene, the poet invents the character of Rosamond, the daughter of Fair Rosamond, whose remains have long lain in a neglected grave beyond the walls of the nunnery.[45] In her, now a novice of the sisterhood, Fair Rosamond lives again in the beauty and innocence that were hers before her fall. From her, too, radiate happiness and benevolence. She knows the sad story of her mother, and the freshly-plucked lilies with which she decorates her grave

[42] In Burnand's version, Eleanor tells Margery's fortune, and receives from her the secret of the labyrinth in return for a promise of further revelations.

[43] In employing so many names here for the various members of Rosamond's household, Baring is probably glancing at the great variety of names used for these stock characters in different versions of the story. It is, incidentally, a curious quirk of the artistic mind that for some reason it feels under compulsion to disguise a borrowed character by changing his name.

[44] Three Short Plays: *Godstow Nunnery, Love in the Desert, Memnon* (London, 1930), pp. 9-26. My thanks are due to Mr. John Masefield, O. M., for calling my attention to this little play.

[45] No other story-teller has assigned a daughter to Fair Rosamond. For an account of Hugh of Lincoln's order that Rosamond's body be removed from the chapel and buried outside the church, see above, pp. 2-3.

were like the thoughts
she had when in the light she was
And had no cause for beauty's sake
and love's, and grief's, to say Alas!

She often imagines her presence in the cloister or the garden walk, and she loves her because "She was unhappy, and beautiful." When widowed Queen Eleanor, old, unhappy, and still tormented by memories of Fair Rosamond, pays a visit to Godstow, it is the beauty and innocence and goodness of Rosamond, the daughter of her hated rival, that revive her humanity and bring her at last to forgiveness and true penitence. Binyon's freshness and his originality in dimming the tragic story of the past to show how innocence and beauty and goodness and truth endure are matched by a dramatic treatment at once simple, decorous, and sincere.

In 1938, Russell G. Pruden published a one-act, blank-verse play titled *Rosamond,*[46] which is marked among other things by the importance given to the rejected lover as the innocent agent by whom Queen Eleanor finds her way through the maze to Rosamond. The action takes place on a June night in "Rosamond's bower near Woodstock." The servants, Will, Tom, and Margaret, apprehensive of danger, suspect a prowler about the maze, and as the king takes his leave of Rosamond to "hunt rebellious sons," he gives her a ring which she is to send him if danger should threaten, and warns her of the designs of the queen. Margaret tells her of a man seen lurking in the shadows of the maze, but Rosamond, though fearful, tries to maintain her calm. Stephen, her youthful lover long ago displaced by Henry, rushes in, and in desperation demands that she go away with him. Disliking all violence, she refuses out of compassion to permit the servants to turn him away. Upon her rejection of his proposal, however, Stephen becomes violent and threatening, but eventually leaves. Will, ordered to follow him at a distance, sees him enter Rufus's Tower, where the queen lodges. Tom is sent posthaste with the ring to King Henry. Thinking that the queen will only banish Rosamond, and that he may then regain her at last, Stephen guides her and her party through the maze to the bower. Warned of the queen's approach, Rosamond forbids all violence and welcomes her. The queen intends that Rosamond shall take her own life:

But it's my whim your own hand do your murder.
Then if the king chides will I say, "My Harry,
Your light-o'-love snuffed out her flame in grief
For a younger lover, comelier than you." (p. 106)

When Rosamond refuses to drink the poison, Stephen is brought in and

[46] In *August Night* (Boston, 1938), pp. 67-122.

threatened with torture. Offered a choice of poison or dagger, Rosamond drinks poison. Henry enters and in his sudden fury mortally wounds Stephen, who before he dies convinces Henry of his innocence and of the queen's treachery. The servants carry him out, and Henry sits down to watch through the night over the dead body of his beloved.

Pruden's use of the servants' conversation to create a feeling of impending danger is a departure from the usual soliloquy of Rosamond, or her dialogue with her maid, for the same purpose. His characterization of Rosamond is fully developed. Although subject to feminine fears, she is yet so courageous and calm that she refuses to flee from her enemies even when opportunity offers, and she is of such a trustful and gentle nature that her dislike of violence in any form causes her to fall victim to Eleanor's threats of torture to the importunate but rebuffed Stephen. As for Stephen himself, he is the rejected rival lover of tradition, of course, but with a significant difference. He does not, like Hawkins's Leicester,[47] for example, repay Rosamond by murdering her father, nor, like D'Agneville,[48] to whom he bears a close resemblance, does he in revenge treacherously conduct Eleanor to Rosamond's bower. What he does is done in desperation and comparative innocence, for he assumes that Eleanor will merely free Rosamond from Henry by banishment, and then he will be able to renew his suit with greater hope of success. The threats of torture to which he is subjected before the eyes of Rosamond, although new as applied to the rival lover, will recall to the reader various earlier instances in nineteenth-century versions, in which Eleanor's inhuman and senseless cruelty is displayed in Rosamond's presence.[49] Pruden so constructs Rosamond's character that to prevent violence to Stephen she drinks the fatal potion. Furthermore, there is no earlier instance in tradition in which Henry himself kills a rival lover on the spot. The sending of the ring to him as a token of Rosamond's danger had been used for a similar purpose in E. Barrington's story, "The King and the Lady."[50]

[47] See above, pp. 75-6.
[48] See above, pp. 46-7.
[49] See above, pp. 61, 66.
[50] See above, p. 64.

CHAPTER VI

RETROSPECT

THE LITERARY versions of the story of Fair Rosamond which have appeared during the present century in the form of narrative poem, drama, novel, and tale are strong evidence that after the three and a half centuries since it was first given artistic treatment, the legend continues to attract the attenion of writers, and to challenge their ingenuity in devising variations upon the theme. In retrospect, its beginning seems simple indeed—the historical fact that King Henry II, although married to Eleanor of Aquitaine, had as his mistress Rosamond de Clifford, who was buried in Godstow Nunnery. It is impossible, of course, to measure the contribution of oral tradition to its development during the period of four centuries in which the old chroniclers kept the simple facts on record and embroidered some of the details by a process of accretion. Some attempt may be made, however, in the light of the evidence available, to reconstruct the genesis of the legend during that period. One is inclined to believe that the imprisonment of Queen Eleanor was the starting-point for the growth of the legend. In point of fact, however, since she was a close prisoner for the entire period covered by the action of the story, no labyrinth for safeguarding Rosamond was necessary, and the queen could have had no opportunity to commit the act which tradition has laid to her charge. But the people, authors of what Robert Fabyan calls "ye comon fame," had heard rumors of Henry's illict affair with Rosamond, and of Eleanor's long imprisonment, and after Rosamond's burial at Godstow, they searched for some causal relationship among these incidents. If Henry had been unfaithful, it follows that the wife would be jealous, and might take measures against her rival, and if the wife had been imprisoned and her rival had died suddenly, it follows that the incarceration was in punishment of some deed which the wife had committed against her enemy. Moreover, what is the explanation of that maze at Woodstock Park? Was it not constructed by King Henry to hide his mistress from a jealous and vengeful wife? But the manner of death inflicted upon Fair Rosamond was something to speculate about, and that the folk imagination conjured up some horrible tortures for the queen's victim can be seen in the story told in *The French Chronicle of London.* The more scholarly records that have survived, however, apparently discounted such stories of horror, for none gives any hint as to the manner of her death. Furthermore, if a great king should fall in love with the most beautiful lady in all the world, what is more natural than that he should give her a rare gift—a marvellous coffer, mysterious in its workings? And if his beloved should suddenly be taken from him, her tomb must of course bear an epitaph. But the curious Latin epitaph which the chroniclers assert was made for Rosamond de Clifford was, of course, none of the folk's devising, for it was undoubtedly transferred by a confused or facetious writer from the tomb of Rosamunda, queen of the Lombards, to the monument at Godstow Abbey. If, moreover, one should need to account for the persistent belief in the poisoned bowl as the cause of Rosamond's death, one may not be far from the truth in assigning its origin to the same source.

Although we have no explicit evidence regarding the nature of the complete story as it may have existed in oral tradition in the time of Queen Elizabeth, we may notice the components of the legend as it had appeared in printed record before William Warner and Samuel Daniel decided to make it the subject of a narrative poem. It is a simple story of how King Henry, although already married to Eleanor of Aquitaine, loved Fair Rosamond, to whom he gave a marvellous casket, and for whom, to protect her from the vengeful hand of his jealous queen, he built at Woodstock an intricate labyrinth in which to conceal her, and of how the queen by some means or other—possibly by following a silken clue—threaded the labyrinth, and so dealt with Fair Rosamond that she died soon thereafter, and was buried at Godstow Nunnery in a tomb on which was inscribed a curious Latin epitaph.

In giving artistic treatment to these materials, Elizabethan writers increased the number of characters and incidents of the story, and more clearly defined both the action and the motivation of the characters. Among the new characters provided are the rival lover who is rejected by Rosamond, the keeper of the bower,[1] a maid who serves as a pandaress, and an agent who acts for Eleanor in bringing about her rival's death. Certain other possibilities for future growth of the story are to be observed in Henry's wooing in disguise, his use of a place for Rosamond's seduction before her removal to the labyrinth at Woodstock, her request to accompany him to France as his page, the increase and variation of the difficulties with which the queen met before she reached Rosamond in her bower, the specific use of poison administered by the queen, and Henry's imprisonment of her for her treacherous act. Furthermore, the same writers cast the story in several

[1] Although in the only version (Warner's) in which a rival lover appears, he is also the keeper of the bower. Later writers sometimes followed this practice, but more often separated the two roles.

different forms, which encouraged variety of treatment. The simple narrative poem, the medieval tragedy with its wailing ghost, and the exchanged poetical epistles were supplemented later by the versified historical romance and the prose chapbook, and each of these, because of its individual formal requirements, treated the story in its own way and added something new to the tradition. Strangely absent from this list, however, is the drama, which apparently gave no more than incidental attention to the legend—and that in only one poor play, *Look about You* (1600). Among the new developments in the first half of the seventeenth century may be mentioned Thomas May's interweaving of the story with the events of Henry's reign, although he brings the love affair into a causal relationship in no wise with the political and religious struggles of the time. The chapbook goes a little farther by making Eleanor's incitement of the rebellion of her sons an act of revenge for Henry's extramarital conduct with Rosamond. It is not until the appearance of John Bancroft's tragedy in 1693, however, that any real attempt was made to bring the more practical problems of the realm to bear directly upon the fortunes of Fair Rosamond. The scope of the story was greatly enlarged by him when he represented the ecclesiastical partisans of the martyred Becket in conspiracy with Queen Eleanor against Henry as king, and against Rosamond as his mistress.

In tracing the early development of the theme, one must not underemphasize the significance of new features introduced into the tradition by the seventeenth-century chapbook, for it was everywhere available, and no doubt it was widely read by all who were interested in the legend. Among other things, it demonstrated to future writers that much could be made of the necessary first meeting of Henry and Rosamond, and of the difficulties which he encountered with her parents and with her resistance to his amorous advances. It enlarged the role both of the rival lover and of the governess, elaborated the intricacy and increased the mystery of the great labyrinth at Woodstock, introduced "death by the sword" as the lethal alternative to poisoning, and made the first reference in a literary version to Rosamond's unborn child. The first dramatization of the story also made some important contributions to the plot. In addition to major changes already referred to, Bancroft represents the queen as being foiled in her first attempt upon Rosamond's life, and he makes the first use of the dream as a warning to Henry that his mistress is in danger. The following century saw important minor innovations in a slight expansion of the older chapbook version by the interpolation of moralizing and historical passages, and of a few fresh borrowings from the drama, in the cultivation of the local poem, and in the introduction of opera and the suggestion of burlesque by Addison.

But Addison at the beginning of the century and Ireland at the end are responsible for major alterations in the whole conception of the story, which were to have a marked effect upon its future development. In his opera *Rosamond* (1707), perhaps as a concession to the skeptical attitude toward "monkish history" or in recognition of an increasing demand for greater historical accuracy, Addison so arranges his plot that the death of the heroine is averted by a sleeping potion, and she is made to retire to the seclusion of a convent. This bold stroke led to considerable inventiveness on the part of later writers, who, like Addison, adopted the idea that for the sake of story-interest Rosamond must be threatened but must at the same time be saved by some means or other from the vengeance of the queen, to live her last days in retirement from the world. Whereas in Addison, the queen administers an innocuous potion in order that Rosamond may be conveyed to a convent, Miller has the queen's own agent omit the poison from the drink without her knowledge. In Hawkins, Rosamond is so frightened by Eleanor's feigned anger and threats of violence that she willingly goes to a convent. Egan, however, has Rosamond's keeper arrive in time to save her from Eleanor and her Saracen slave. A nineteenth-century chapbook makes Rosamond's meekness and beauty completely subdue the evil intentions of the queen. In Maberly, Becket's cruel persecution of Rosamond forces her to seek refuge in a nunnery. The good Eleanor of Smith's version prevails over her rival by gentle persuasion. Wightwick avoids the entire problem by beginning his play after Rosamond's retirement to a convent. Tennyson's Becket arrives in time to save Rosamond from Eleanor's dagger, and to convey her to Godstow Nunnery.

Another important change, which resulted in further complication of the story, was Ireland's introduction of Becket. The way had been prepared for this move by Bancroft's and Hull's use of Becket's partisans in their conspiracy with the queen against Henry and Rosamond. In Ireland's play, Becket represents the same sort of opposition, but he yields reluctantly to the practice of treachery. In the nineteenth-century he was conceived by a number of dramatists as a figure about whom a drama might be made to revolve,[2] and his character in the Rosamond story underwent a number of variations until it reached its most admirable proportions in Tennyson. Thomas Miller, for example, in 1839 created a Becket radically different from the conspirator of Ireland's play by revealing him as an encourager of the illicit love affair, and as a protector of Fair Rosamond, who in turn attempts the role of peacemaker between him and King Henry. In the following year Darley presented a Becket who loved pomp and gay living, and who not only defended the pair of lovers against the queen's suspicion

[2] See above, p. 84.

and prying, but refused to aid her in her schemes against her rival. In Maberly's novel, on the other hand, Becket is made the rejected lover, who, meeting with a rebuff from Rosamond, persecutes her unmercifully. In 1863 Hamilton shows only a vestige of this idea by having Becket confess that he had been Rosamond's youthful lover before Henry seduced her. Tennyson's Becket, developed as the character was from Miller's novel, is the friend and protector of Rosamond even to the point of incurring death in performing that duty, imposed by royal command, and by his own sympathy for the unfortunate girl. As a character, curiously enough, he begins as a villain in Ireland's play, and in less than a century later he ends as a victim of circumstance and of his faithfulness to duty in preserving the weak from oppression.

The introduction and transformation of this character are but two of several marked innovations occurring in the nineteenth century. The story was given greater scope and variety by its incorporation into the historical novel, by the appearance of burlesque and pantomime, and by the rise and continued popularity of the one-act play. The historical romances and plays in the middle years of the century introduced such new plot-devices as the raid, the abduction, and the elopement; a considerable amount of feudal life and history; incidents designed to reveal Queen Eleanor's cruelty; and the king's disguise and secret marriage handled in a variety of ways to alter the course of the action. Other innovations were supernatural and grotesque elements—ghosts and conjurers and fairies and witches—and the integration of songs into the plays, as in Swinburne, Grindrod, and Tennyson. By some writers the number of rival lovers is increased together with both the nature and quantity of their villainy practiced against Rosamond; a greater number of historical characters, such as Prince Eustace, and many semi-historical characters are brought into the story; and the two children, Geoffrey and William, are employed in a number of ways to increase the variety and interest of the plot. Caricature of the story, the first hints of which are to be seen in Addison's opera and in other writings of the preceding century, was fully developed in pantomime and in burlesque plays by Thomas Proclus Taylor, Sir Francis Cowley Burnand, Frederick Langbridge, and others in the popular theaters of London. These brief pieces, together with the widely-read *Dramatic Scenes* of Mary Russell Mitford, did much to reveal the possibilities of the theme for both serious and burlesque treatment in thc onc-act play.

Two departures from the traditional conception of the legend deserve special attention, because they reveal both the liberty which authors are free to take with the story, and the fecundity of the legend in providing new growths. George Wightwick's *Henry the Second* (1851) omits the love affair between Henry and Rosamond, and begins his action after her retirement to Godstow Abbey. He assigns to the pair a son never heard of before—one Sir Walter Clifford—and introduces Princess Alice as the comforter of the king in his loneliness, and as the beloved of Sir Walter. In his *Godstow Nunnery* (1930) Laurence Binyon begins his action long after the death of Fair Rosamond at Godstow, and assigns to her daughter by Henry, also named Rosamond, the role of bringing the aged widow Queen Eleanor to penitence and forgiveness.

These radical departures from common practice raise certain related questions concerning the different attitudes and interests shown by various authors in dealing with the characters and incidents of the story. What features of the story as it stood in the earliest stages of its literary development were rejected or gradually discarded? What features appear to have attracted most attention or to have called forth the greatest effort at ingenuity to produce variations of pattern? The marvellous little casket or coffer, which is given special attention in the accounts of the chroniclers, is ignored by Warner but is artistically employed by Daniel and Drayton as an aid in the seduction of Rosamond. It is then completely dropped by all succeeding writers, with the very recent exception of John Masefield. The epitaph, which, like the coffer, received careful treatment in the chronicles, is reduced to a faint allusion in Warner and Daniel, and to an English paraphrase of the original Latin in the chapbook, and is thereafter rarely mentioned. A number of other devices may be treated as short-lived innovations, which were used but once or, sporadically, but a few times through the years—for example, Henry's wooing in disguise, Rosamond's request to accompany him to France as his page, her use of the planet-book, the ominous dream, the consultation of a conjurer, the appearance of Rosamond's ghost at the funeral of Becket, the gift of a ring or cross as a token of Henry's affection or as a device to be used by Rosamond when danger threatens. There are, of course, many less striking ones. Some of these were not accepted by succeeding writers; others were perhaps too representative of the peculiar taste of the individual author or of his age to appeal to later writers, or were used too late in the tradition for us to judge at this time of their longevity.

Some features of the story remain unchanged, or change but a single time, throughout the tradition. Whenever violent death is not averted by some means or other, fair Rosamond always dies of poison administered by the queen or by her command. The alternative of death by the dagger, first introduced in the seventeenth-century chapbook or in Bancroft's play, is never once resorted to by her or inflicted upon her by her rival. Although numerous attempts are made to stab her, not once is her blood shed. Moreover, save in one instance—in Ranking's *Fair Rosamond* (1868), where she forsakes her first love, Hugh of

Endisley, for King Henry—Rosamond is never fickle in her love. Although she many times receives declarations of love from other men, she remains without exception true to King Henry. One is inclined to surmise that her beauty and her position as the unfortunate victim of a royal lover have somehow given her a sort of sanctity and inviolability in the eyes of all writers who have told her story. On the other hand, Eleanor is almost invariably represented as suspicious, jealous, vengeful, relentless, and, in versions of the last century, cruel to others than her rival without cause. It is true that in Addison's opera she used an innocent sleeping-potion instead of poison, and in Hawkins she only feigned violence, according to her report, and succeeded in frightening Rosamond into a convent, yet in only one version of the story is she ever a good woman—a gentle, generous, and understanding wife who knows neither hate nor jealousy, but successfully uses persuasion to induce her rival to retire to Godstow Nunnery.[3]

Certain characters and devices introduced into the earliest literary versions appear with varying degrees of regularity, but, of course, with modifications throughout the tradition: Eleanor's agent, the rival lover, the keeper of the bower, Rosamond's maid; the labyrinth, Rosamond's burial at Godstow, promised or actual imprisonment of the queen. In the last century, too, the first meeting of the lovers, the secret marriage, and the two children of Henry and Rosamond appear to have attracted steady attention. It is upon some of these features of the story that writers seem to have exercised most ingenuity in producing variations either by combining or interchanging various roles, or by instituting some minor alteration at a critical point in the action which markedly alters the remainder of the story. A brief sketch of the development of a few of the more important of them may not be out of place here. In William Warner, who deserves credit for inventing the roles, the keeper of the bower, or the "Knight of trust," seeks Rosamond's love in vain. This brief mention of the rival lover was not exploited by any writer until half-a-century later, when he was given much attention by the earliest chapbook in an independent role as a lord who has the paternal blessing. Addison, however, like Warner, combines the roles of keeper and rival lover—although the character is not to be taken seriously—but Hawkins is the first to make the rival lover, in the person of Leicester, a villain who conspires against the king and kills Rosamond's father. Actually the role of the rejected rival lover does not develop fully until well into the nineteenth century. John Barnett's opera, *Fair Rosamond* (1837), provides two rival lovers, Sir Aubrey De Vere, who, as in the chapbook, is betrothed to Rosamond, and Raymond De Burgh, who, upon his rejection, becomes Eleanor's agent and leads her to the bower. Of the two spurned lovers in Egan's novel, Prince Eustace at-

[3] See John Frederick Smith, above, pp. 59-61.

tempts to defame Rosamond, and Le Gros joins the queen in conspiracy against her. In *The History of Fair Rosamond* (1846?) the older and more conventional lover, Lord Fitzwarren, who is betrothed to Rosamond, takes no action, though D'Agneville, architect and keeper of the bower, reveals to Eleanor the secret of the labyrinth. Maberly inaugurates a radical departure when Becket, upon Rosamond's refusal of his love, resorts to persecution of her, whereas Ranulph de Broc, in contrast, loves on to the end, and finally avenges her by participating in the murder of her oppressor. In Winspere's play the principle of contrast is again employed, when Robin Roughhead saves Rosamond from death by rendering her drink harmless, and Hereford, seeking by a trick to abduct her from Godstow Nunnery, is killed for his pains. Tennyson goes so far as to make three of the knights who murdered Becket rejected lovers of Rosamond. Clara Turnbull, curiously enough, makes Eleanor mistake Fredègonda, the female knight, as a lover of Rosamond. In E. O. Browne's novel Prince Eustace turns villain in revenge, but Sir Richard de Gifford, as a loyal friend of King Henry, must suffer in silence and finally conduct Fair Rosamond to Godstow Nunnery. A still further ingenious variation of the role is to be found in Pruden's *Fair Rosamond* (1938) where Stephen, the still hopeful but desperate lover, innocently leads the queen through the maze to Rosamond. From among all these variations certain patterns emerge, which result from combining the roles of rejected lover and keeper of the bower, making him remain loyal as a contrast to a villainous rival, or causing him to seek revenge by joining with the queen to commit some outrage against Rosamond or her father. The use of the revenge motive is prominent in nineteenth-century versions of the story.

The role of keeper of the bower is so frequently combined with that of the rival lover from the very beginning that the discussion of the one has involved much of the other. In two versions—the early chapbook and Faucit's play—he is Rosamond's uncle, in Bancroft's tragedy he is self-styled "the king's pimp," because the duties of the original procuress are transferred to him, and in Tennyson's *Becket* he is a historical figure, John of Salisbury, who serves in the capacity of tutor as well. An interesting character was developed from the keeper of the bower. In the early versions, especially in those of Drayton and Deloney, it is emphasized that he is the king's closest friend, in whom is placed absolute trust. The friendship theme, however, was not exploited until much later, when, in Egan and Winspere, and more recently in Browne, Henry's faithful friend, although no longer the keeper except in Winspere, becomes one of the most attractive additions to the story. In Browne's version, for example, the role of faithful friend is combined with that of rival lover, and these are maintained, strangely enough with plausibility, to the end of the story.

The part of Rosamond's female companion also undergoes an interesting change in development. The procuress invented by Daniel is continued by Drayton and May, and given even more attention in the earliest chapbook version. Later, however, she discards her evil duties to become a maid or companion to Rosamond, often characterless, at times suspicious of and unwelcome to her mistress. It is as if writers inherited her and sometimes seemed hardly to know how to use her to advantage. Indeed, in a few instances, her original role is transferred to a man. The reason for her loss of the original role of procuress is not far to seek. Once writers had learned, especially in the nineteenth century, what varied results could be made to follow a secret marriage, real or faked, before or after Henry's union with Eleanor, pandering and seduction were no longer necessary to the plot. It should be pointed out that in no instance does Rosamond's maid ever openly betray her, with the possible exception of Swinburne's Constance, although the poet is not clear on the point. On the other hand, in E. Barrington's little story, Petronille even deceives the queen and lends aid to Henry and Rosamond in evading the wife's prying. Almost every writer, in the case of the maid as in that of other stock figures, feels the necessity of altering her name, as if to cover up his source or as if the change would somehow help to produce something new.

Lord Walter de Clifford, though not present in all versions of the story, is so differently handled in the tradition that one is led to assume that most writers had difficulty in giving him a role that could be consistently justified. He first appears in the earliest chapbook version as the father who favors the match between Rosamond and Lord Fitzwalters and does what he can to protect her from the bold and persistent attentions of King Henry. This part of his role is used later in no version except Egan's. He next appears in Hawkins as the father who is determined to trap Leicester—the villain who is in love with Rosamond—but he himself is slain in the attempt. In Hull he laments the loss of his daughter to Henry's lust, and plans to convey her to a convent, but Eleanor arrives at Woodstock before him, and poisons her. Rosamond's secret marriage in Miller so shocks the old man that he makes a pilgrimage to the Holy Land—an idea repeated and enlarged in Maberly. In Egan's novel he is misled by Prince Eustace to think his daughter is loose with Henry, but is relieved to find her married to him. In Ireland's play he is taken prisoner by the queen for no reason at all, and in Darley he advises Rosamond to seek the king's protection against Eleanor's jealousy, and not to go to Godstow, as she had planned to do. In Browne he is made a gruff, cruel, and unscrupulous character to whom principle means nothing where personal advantage is in prospect. There is, then, no development here, no evolution of the character. He is unable to find a convincing, even if conventional, role in the story to which he seems to have belonged, and very few writers use him to any great advantage.

Perhaps writers reveal their greatest ingenuity in devising variations on the means by which the queen manages to thread the maze in order to reach Rosamond in her bower. In the early literary versions much is made of the intricacy of the labyrinth, but in the eighteenth century it is almost ignored, perhaps as too improbable for a somewhat matter-of-fact age, only to be revived, in the last century, in descriptions which render belief in its existence much more acceptable, and which lead to emphasis upon the increased difficulty which Eleanor had in learning and mastering its secret. In Warner and Deloney the knight who guards the bower is overpowered, and the guiding clue is taken from him, although in Daniel the thread is left by chance, and Eleanor and her confederates find it. These inventions set the pattern for many of the later versions. In some instances the keeper is killed, or is diverted by a false message sent by a postboy, or is tricked by Eleanor and her agent in disguise. In others the clue is snatched from Rosamond, or from her maid, or Rosamond's child innocently leads the queen through the maze to his mother. In one version the keeper is also a rival lover, D'Agneville, in the *History of Fair Rosamond,* who avenges his rejection in love by revealing the secret to the queen. Sir Richard de Gifford, in Browne's novel, who has long loved Rosamond without encouragement, is persuaded by Eleanor that the secret door is the work of the king's enemies, and is prevailed upon to break it down. Another rejected lover, Pruden's Stephen, also in innocence, leads the queen to the bower because he thinks she will banish Rosamond, and so make her more receptive to his suit. In Swinburne the queen's lover shows her the way. From the earliest instances of the thread caught in Henry's spur, originally used merely to arouse the queen's suspicion, are developed various devices, such as snatching the thread from his spur as he comes out of the labyrinth, unrolling a ball of thread attached to his spur while he treads the maze, and the queen's laying down the clue as she follows the king or some other person who has access to the bower. The original clue of thread is often used, although the device of personal contact is employed by other writers to complicate the action. Sometimes the queen takes advantage of the absence or sickness of the keeper, who has left the bower unguarded. In a number of versions, however, the problem does not arise; in others, no specific account is offered.

Finally, what generalizations may be made regarding the various forms which have been preferred by authors since Elizabethan times? What can be said of the attitude of writers toward the tradition which each in his own way was helping to perpetuate? The narrative poem with which the story was introduced to Elizabethan readers was eventually pretty largely superseded by the drama and the novel. These forms were perhaps better suited to a story, which, although it was simple at the start, and in its essential elements continued to be so, became increasingly complicated by the introduction of new characters and of backgrounds of political and religious events and feudal life in general. Of the two forms prefered in the last century-and-a-half, the drama and the novel, the former has been much more frequently cultivated and has been given more varied treatment. As for the second question—the attitude of writers toward the tradition—it is clear from the evidence, I believe, that from the later years of the seventeenth century, authors have been, almost to a man, clearly conscious of a long literary tradition behind them, but have turned in most instances to two or more earlier versions of the Rosamond story for suggestions—versions which were very often not older than a generation or two. Most writers have a care not to follow their sources in servile fashion, and the best of them usually seize upon some salient feature of the story, and by altering it slightly, they manage to give the plot the effect of novelty and originality. If this study of the development of an old theme through the years demonstrates anything, it is that a simple story of love and jealousy and death may be periodically renewed by the skill of competent craftsmen, and thus need never cease to prove its attraction to writer and reader alike through successive generations.

INDEX[1]

Addison, Joseph, 30, 48, 52, 61, 72-5, 76-7, 82, 88, 94, 95, 97, 106, 123, 124, 125, 127
Akhurst, W. M., 83
Archex, T. A., 2
Arnold, Samuel, 77
Ashton, John, 39

Bancroft, John, 39, 45, 47, 50, 52, 69-72, 74, 75, 79, 81, 82, 86, 89, 100, 103, 111, 123, 126, 128
Baring, Maurice, 117-18
Barnett, John, 88-9, 95, 98, 113, 127
Barrington, E. (Mrs. Lilly Adams Beck), 63-4, 120, 129
Beck, Lilly Adams. See Barrington, E.
Bedfod, Countess of, 20
Benedict, Abbot of Peterborough, 2
Benington, Joseph, 2
Binyon, Laurence, 84, 118-19, 126
Bradley, Katherine Harris. See Field, Michael
Brand, John, 33-4
Brandon, Dorothy, 63
Brompton, John, 6
Browne, E. O., 64-7, 128, 129, 130
Burnand, Francis Cowley, 82, 94-6, 97, 113, 117, 125
Burton, Robert, 28

Camden, William, 7
Campbell, Lady Archibald, 107
Campion, Thomas, 28
Capes, Bernard, 61-2 66
Carr, T. A., 83
Carte, Thomas, 2
Cattermole, Richard, 84
Churchyard, Thomas, 15, 17, 19, 20
Chute, Anthony, 20
Coleman, George, 78
Coleridge, Samuel Taylor, 34
Cooper, Edith Emma. See Field, Michael
Cooper, John Gilbert, 30
Corio Bernardino, 8
Cother, T., 82

Daniel, Samuel, 12, 14, 15, 16-20, 21, 23, 24, 27, 32, 38, 42, 47, 71, 75, 108, 122, 126, 129, 130
Darley, George, 62, 66, 89-92, 98, 103, 109, 112, 124, 129
"Death of Fair Rosamond," 36
Deloney, Thomas, 22-3, 27, 42-3, 45, 49, 71, 79, 87, 116, 128, 130
De Vere, Aubrey Thomas, 84
Dickens, Charles, 59
Donne, John, 71
Drayton, Michael, 7, 20-1, 27, 28, 32, 34, 37, 42, 49, 71, 75, 126, 128, 129
Dryden, John, 69
Dugdale, Sir William, 29, 49

Ebsworth, Joseph W., 31
Edward III, *King of England,* 4, 5
Egan, Pierce, 53-6, 59, 61, 66, 67, 95, 98, 106, 107, 124, 128, 129
Eleanor of Provence, 10
Eliot, T. S., 84
Ellis, Brandon, 83
Eyton, Robert William, 2

Fabyan, Robert, 6, 7, 11, 121
Fair Rosamond, 82
Fair Rosamond; or, *The Bower of Woodstock,* 44ff.
Fair Rosamond to the Fair Hibernian, 33
Fall of Fair Rosamond, 82
Faucit, John Saville, 84-6, 95, 128
Ferne, Sir John, 2
Field, Michael (*pseud.* for Katherine Harris Bradley and Edith Emma Cooper), 113-15
Fletcher, Giles, *the Elder,* 20
Fletcher, Phineas, 28
French Chronicle of London, 10, 11, 12, 18, 43, 121
Fuller, Thomas, 29

Genest, John, 69-70, 75, 76
George II, *King of England,* 75
Giraldus Cambrensis, 2, 6
Godwin, Edward William, 107
Grafton, Richard, 7
Greene, Robert, 32, 42

[1] Persons, places, and fictional devices which appear in the story are not included in this index.

Grindrod, Charles, 102-04, 117, 125

Hamilton, Alexander, 84, 125
Harrison, William, 30
Hawkins, William, 48, 75-7, 79, 81, 82, 106, 120, 124, 127, 129
Hearne, Thomas, 29
Helps, Sir Arthur, 84
Henry I, *King of England*, 45
Henry III, *King of England*, 10
Heywood, Thomas, 24
Higden, Ranulf, 6, 7, 8, 9, 11, 12, 18
History of Fair Rosamond, the Beautiful Mistress of King Henry the Second, 46-8, 105, 128, 130
History of Fair Rosamond, otherwise Eleanor Clifford, 44ff.
History of the Life and Death of Fair Rosamond, 44ff.
Holinshed, Raphael, 7, 11, 23, 60
Hookes, Nicholas, 28
Hugh, *Bishop of Lincoln, Saint*, 1, 2
Hull, Thomas, 50, 60, 75, 77-9, 81, 82, 86, 89, 103, 129
Hume, Davis, 2

Ireland, William Henry, 50, 53, 58, 79-82, 89, 90, 91, 124, 125, 129
Irving, Sir Henry, 108

Jerrold, Douglas, 84

Knighton, Henry, 6

Langbridge, Frederick, 96-7, 125
Larpent, John, 84
Leatherdale, The Rev. Vincent John. See Winspere, John
Leland, John, 8, 9
Life and Death of Fair Rosamond, 31, 39-46, 85
Lightfoot, Joseph Barber, *Bishop*, 109
Lodge, Oliver W. F., 116-17
Lodge, Thomas, 20
Look about You, 23-4, 38, 52, 123
"The Loves of King Henry II, and Fair Rosamond," 44ff.
Lupino, George, 82
Lyttelton, George, *Baron*, 2, 76

Maberly, Kate Charlotte, 56-9, 67, 95, 98, 107, 124, 125, 128, 129
Macklin, F. H., 107
MacCready, William Charles, 98
Mary I, *Queen of England*, 13
Masefield, John, 28, 36-7, 118, 126
Matthews, W. H., 5
May, Thomas, 24-7, 38, 39, 42, 47, 71, 75, 123, 129
Meres, Francis, 20
Miller, Thomas, 47, 50-3, 54, 55, 56, 59, 61, 67, 91, 92, 95, 98, 106, 109, 111-12, 124, 125, 129
Millet, Maud, 107
Mitford, Mary Russell, 35, 53, 86-7, 116, 117, 125
Morris, William, 100
Mountfort, William, 69

Nashe, Thomas, 19
Neville, Josephine, 83
Nield, Jonathan, 63

Oldmixon, John, 28

Parker, Henry, 11
Pattison, William, 32, 103
Paulus Diaconus, 8
Payne, W. H., 82
Percy, Thomas, *Bishop*, 79, 86, 115, 116
Philip II, *King of Spain*, 13
Phillips, Kate, 108
Pocock, Isaac, 84
Pope, Alexander, 29-30
Pruden, Russell G., 119-20, 128, 130
Pye, Henry James, 83-4

"Queen Eleanor's Confession," 49

Ranking, B. Montgomerie, 34-6, 126-7
Robert of Gloucester, 4
Roe, Bassett, 107
Rosamunda, Queen of the Lombards, 8, 9, 122
Rossetti, Dante Gabriel, 100
Rowe, Nicholas, 78

Saville, John. See Faucit, John Saville
Scott, Sir Walter, 48, 50, 67
Scott, William Bell, 34
Shakespeare, William, 79
Shenstone, William, 77, 79
Shetson, Erroll, 83
Shore, Jane, 17, 19, 28
Slatyer (Slater), Thomas, 24
Smith, John Frederick, 58-61, 107, 124
Soutar, Robert, 83
Speed, John, 11

Spenser, Edmund, 20
Stephen, *King of England,* 45
Strickland, Agnes, 3, 5
Swinburne, Algernon Charles, 98, 100-01, 113, 117, 125, 129, 130

Taylor, Thomas, 93
Taylor, Thomas Proclus, 93-4, 125
Tennyson, Alfred, 53, 62, 63, 66, 92, 107-13, 115, 124, 125, 128
Terriss, W., 108
Terry, Ellen, 108
Tickell, Thomas, 30
Trevisa, John de, 6, 8, 9
Turnbull, Clara, 62-3, 128

Unfortunate Concubine, 31, 41-2, 49
Unfortunate Concubines, 44ff.
Unfortunate Royal Mistresses, 48-9

Waites, Alfred, 84
Wallis, C. E., 83
Ward, Genevieve, 107, 108
Warner, William, 12, 13-16, 17, 18, 21, 23, 27, 35, 38, 43, 71, 87, 122, 126, 127, 130
Warton, Thomas, 4
Wendell, Barrett, 115-16
Wightwick, George, 98-100, 107, 124, 125
Wildfrau Story, 12-13, 37
Winspere, John (i.e., Vincent John Leatherdale), 61, 97, 98, 104-06, 128
Wood, Anthony à, 29

NORTHWESTERN UNIVERSITY
The Graduate School
1947

From time to time, The Graduate School of Northwestern University authorizes through the Editorial Board of *Northwestern University Studies* the publication of monographs in various fields of learning. A list of these publications appears below. Orders and inquiries are to be addressed to The Graduate School, Northwestern University, Evanston, Illinois.

Northwestern University Studies in the Humanities

No. 1. *Tales from the French Folk Lore of Missouri* by Joseph Médard Carrière $4.00
No. 2. *Kant's Pre-Critical Ethics* by Paul Arthur Schilpp $2.50
No. 3. *Luise Hensel als Dichterin* by Frank Spiecker
No. 4. *The Labors of the Months in Antique and Mediaeval Art* by James Carson Webster $10.00
No. 5. *Forgotten Danteiana* by J. G. Fucilla $1.00
No. 6. *Speech Development of a Bilingual Child* by Werner F. Leopold $2.25
No. 7. *L'Histoire de Gille de Chyn* edited by Edwin B. Place $2.50
No. 8. *The Aesthetic Process* by Bertram Morris $2.25
No. 9. *The Classical Republicans* by Zera S. Fink $4.00
No. 10. *An Historical and Analytical Bibliography of the Literature of Cryptology* by Joseph S. Galland $5.00
No. 11. *Speech Development of a Bilingual Child, Volume II* by Werner F. Leopold $5.50
No. 12. *Bibliography of the Published Writings of John Mill* by Ney MacMinn and others $2.50
No. 13. *Political Forgiveness in Old Athens* by Alfred P. Dorjahn $1.50
No. 14. *Education for Journalism in the United States from Its Beginning to 1940* by Albert Alton Sutton $2.00
No. 15. *Analytical Syllogistics: A Pragmatic Interpretation of the Aristotelian Logic* by Delton Thomas Howard $4.00
No. 16. *Fair Rosamond. A Study of the Development of a Literary Theme* by Virgil B. Heltzel $3.00

Northwestern University Studies in the Social Sciences

No. 1. *Predicting Criminality* by Ferris F. Laune $1.50
No. 2. *Shamanism in Western North America* by Willard Z. Park $2.25
No. 3. *Seventy Years of Real Estate Subdividing in the Region of Chicago* by Helen Corbin Monchow $2.25
No. 4. *The First Scientific Exploration of Russian America and the Purchase of Alaska* by James Alton James $2.00
No. 5. *Compulsory Health Insurance in the United States* by Herbert D. Simpson $ .75

Northwestern University Studies in Mathematics and the Physical Sciences

No. 1. *Mathematical Monographs* by D. R. Curtiss, H. T. Davis, H. L. Garabedian, H. S. Wall, E. D. Hellinger $2.25

Northwestern University Studies in the Biological Sciences and Medicine

No. 1. *A Study in Neotropical Pselaphidæ* by Orlando Park $7.50
No. 2. *A Catalog of Illinois Algae* by Max E. Britton $3.00

Not in series
Galileo: Two New Sciences translated by Henry Crew and Alfonso de Salvio $3.50

Remittances should be made payable to Northwestern University, and should be sent with orders to The Graduate School, Northwestern University, Evanston, Illinois

Prices include postage